The Workload
of the
Supreme
Court

Gerhard Casper

Richard A. Posner

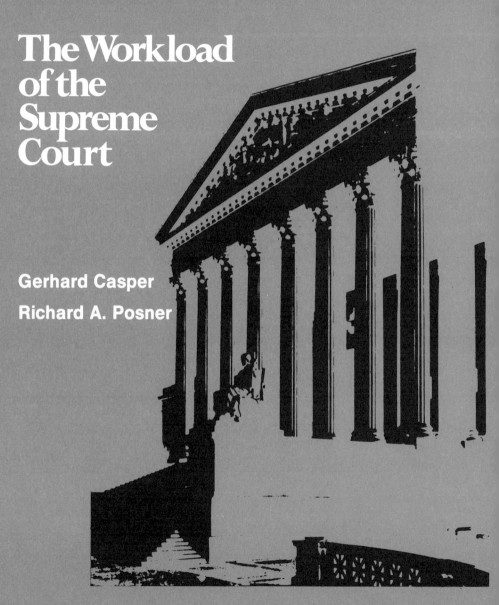

American Bar Foundation

The Workload
of the
Supreme
Court

The Workload of the Supreme Court

Gerhard Casper

Richard A. Posner

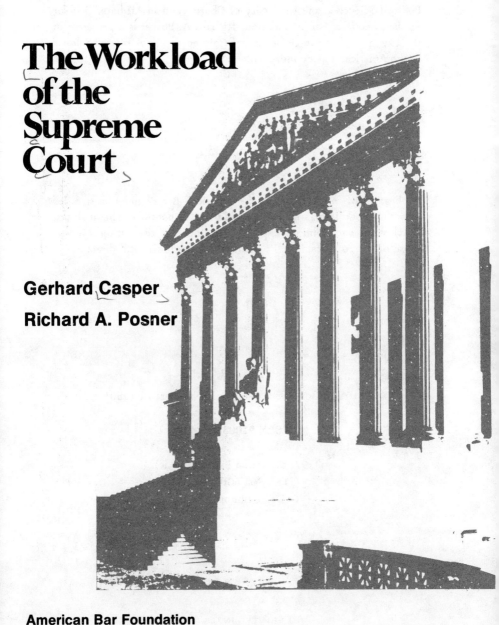

American Bar Foundation
Chicago
1976

Gerhard Casper is a professor in the Law School and the Department of Political Science at the University of Chicago and an Affiliated Scholar of the American Bar Foundation. Richard A. Posner is a professor in the Law School at the University of Chicago and an Affiliated Scholar of the American Bar Foundation.

Library of Congress Catalog Card Number: 76-49801

ISBN 910058-78-4

©1976 American Bar Foundation
1155 East 60th Street
Chicago, Illinois 60637

201829

CONTENTS

LIST OF TABLES

LIST OF FIGURES

PREFACE

In December 1972 a distinguished study group on the caseload of the Supreme Court, under the chairmanship of Professor Paul Freund, recommended a number of changes, some drastic, in the jurisdiction of the United States Supreme Court.[1] These changes were designed to alleviate what the study group believed, partly on the basis of statistics showing a steep and seemingly inexorable increase in the number of applications for Supreme Court review, to be a workload that was too heavy for the good of the Court and the legal system.

The report of the study group touched off a considerable controversy with respect to the gravity of the workload problem and appropriate measures to cope with it.[2]

---

1. See Federal Judicial Center Report of the Study Group on the Case Load of the Supreme Court (Paul A. Freund, chairman) (Admin. Office U.S. Cts. for Fed. Jud. Center, Dec. 1972).

2. The major contributions to the debate at this writing are William H. Alsup, A Policy Assessment of the National Court of Appeals, 25 Hastings L.J. 1313 (1974); Alexander M. Bickel, The Caseload of the Supreme Court—and What, If Anything, to Do About It (Washington, D.C.: Domestic Affairs Study 21, American Enterprise Institute for Public Policy Research, 1973); Charles L. Black, Jr., The National Court of Appeals: An Unwise Proposal, 83 Yale L.J. 883 (1974); William J. Brennan, Jr., The National Court of Appeals: Another Dissent, 40 U. Chi. L. Rev. 473 (1973); Gerhard Casper & Richard A. Posner, A Study of the Supreme Court's Caseload, 3 J. Leg. Studies 339 (1974); Commission on Revision of the Federal Court Appellate System, Structure and Internal Procedures: Recommendations for Change (Washington, D.C., June 1975) [hereinafter cited as Hruska Commission]; Paul A. Freund, Why We Need the National Court of Appeals, 59 A.B.A.J. 247 (1973), and his A National Court of Appeals, 25 Hastings L.J. 1301 (1974); Henry J. Friendly, Averting the Flood by Lessening the Flow, 59 Cornell L. Rev. 634 (1974); Eugene Gressman, The National Court of Appeals: A Dissent, 59 A.B.A.J. 253 (1973); Erwin N. Griswold, The Supreme Court's Case Load: Civil Rights and Other Problems, 1973 U. Ill. L.F. 615, and his Rationing Justice—the Supreme Court's Caseload and What the Court Does Not Do, 60 Cornell L. Rev. 335 (1975); Clement F. Haynsworth, Jr., A New Court to Improve the Administration of Justice, 59 A.B.A.J. 841 (1973); Shirley M. Hufstedler, Courtship and Other Legal Arts, 60 A.B.A.J. 545 (1974); Philip B. Kurland, Jurisdiction of the United States Supreme Court: Time for a Change? 59 Cornell L. Rev. 616 (1974); Douglas A. Poe, John R. Schmidt, & Wayne W. Whalen, Critique: A National Court of Appeals: A Dissenting View, 67 Nw. U.L. Rev. 842 (1973); William H. Rehnquist, Whither the Courts, 60 A.B.A.J. 787 (1974); Earl Warren, Let's Not Weaken the Supreme Court, 60 A.B.A.J. 677 (1974). See also Henry J. Friendly, Federal Jurisdiction: A General View (New York: Columbia University Press, 1973), especially at 47-54.

We entered the fray in June 1974 with the publication of
an article that questioned the radical proposals for jurisdictional change then on the table (including those of the
study group), while attempting a more detailed study of
the relevant statistical evidence than had been attempted by
either the study group or its critics.[3]

The controversy has not abated. Although the specific
proposals of the study group have receded from attention,
other equally drastic proposals have come to the fore,
notably those of the Commission on Revision of the
Federal Court Appellate System.[4] The persistence and
public importance of the controversy over the Supreme
Court's workload have encouraged us to expand and update
our 1974 study. As in the original article, the emphasis in
this monograph is on the statistics of the Supreme Court's
workload. Both our analysis and the statistical data upon
which it is based have been substantially expanded. Since
statistical analysis cannot alone resolve the issues of public
policy raised by the workload controversy, we have also
devoted considerable attention to nonquantitative consider-
ations.

Inevitably, in view of the controversial nature of the
workload question, our study will be viewed primarily as a
contribution to a public policy debate. However, it may
also have value as a contribution to the sparse but growing
literature that uses the methods of the social sciences to
study legal phenomena such as judicial activity in a system-
atic and empirical fashion.

Both the present monograph and the earlier article out
of which it grew were commissioned by the American Bar
Foundation and supported by a grant to the Foundation
from the American Bar Endowment. We gratefully acknowl-
edge the assistance of the Foundation—and the strong
encouragement given our project by the Executive Director
of the Foundation, Spencer L. Kimball. In addition, Charles

3. Casper & Posner, *supra* note 2.
4. See Hruska Commission, *supra* note 2.

Haines and Emilie and Paul Pritchard provided indispensable research assistance, as did a number of other University of Chicago Law School students: Alan Blankenheimer, Holly Davis, Judy Jacobs, Mark Rosenbaum, and Jeffrey Shamis. Marnie Berkowitz of the University of Chicago Law School's Law and Economics Program also provided us with helpful research assistance, and the Law and Economics Program helped us defray other research and clerical costs. We also wish to thank Yakov Avichai, Spencer L. Kimball, Philip B. Kurland, William M. Landes, Geoffrey R. Stone, and Hans Zeisel for their comments on the drafts of our original article, John Saxon and Russell R. Wheeler of the staff of the Supreme Court for assistance in obtaining certain of the data used in this study, and the members of the Office of the Clerk of the Court for the many courtesies that they extended to our research assistants.

CHAPTER 1
INTRODUCTION

The jurisdiction of the typical appellate court is obligatory in the sense that the court is under a duty to decide on the merits any appeal filed with it that comes within its jurisdiction. The Supreme Court of the United States is atypical in this respect (as in many others). Its jurisdiction is for the most part a discretionary one. Most cases in the Supreme Court are commenced by the filing of a petition for a writ of certiorari, which is simply a request that the Court exercise its discretion to decide the case on the merits. If the petition is granted, the case is then set for briefing and argument on the merits.

Some cases are commenced by the filing of an appeal rather than a petition for writ of certiorari. As to these cases the Supreme Court's jurisdiction is formally obligatory, but in fact the Court frequently treats the filing of an appeal as a request for review which it feels free to deny as if the case were before it on certiorari. The jurisdiction that is obligatory in form is discretionary in fact, and the initial filing in an appeal—the "jurisdictional statement"—is the practical equivalent of a petition for certiorari.[1] Thus it would be only a slight exaggeration to describe the entire jurisdiction of the Supreme Court as discretionary. How this came to be so is the subject of chapter 2.

As a consequence of the Court's discretionary jurisdiction, there are two types of decision-making by the Court that enter into computations of its workload. The first consists of its screening of applications for review—whether petitions for certiorari or jurisdictional statements—of which thousands are now filed with the Court each year. Unless otherwise indicated, the terms "cases" and "caseload," as we use them, refer to the applications

---

1. However, dismissal of an appeal, unlike denial of certiorari, does possess at least some precedential value. See, *e.g.,* Hicks v. Miranda, 422 U.S. 332 (1975).

for review that are filed with the Court. The second category of the Court's workload consists of the much smaller number of cases that the Court, having accepted them for review, decides, normally after oral argument, on the merits and with an opinion. This number is within the Court's own control and has, as we shall see, grown but little over the years. The first figure is not within the Court's control—not directly, anyway—and it has grown dramatically over the years, as shown in table 1.1 and figures 1 and 2.[2]

Since the number of applications for review has fluctuated considerably from year to year as indicated by the solid line in figures 1 and 2, a ten-year moving average has been used to "smooth" the raw data and highlight trends of more than a few years' duration. The beaded line in figures 1 and 2 illustrates the relatively stable progression of the ten-year average. Table 1.2 presents a summary by decade of both the average number of cases filed and the average annual rate of change in the ten-year moving

---

2. Our source in table 1.1 and figures 1 and 2 for the number of filings in the period 1880-1913 was the U.S. Attorney General's annual reports for those years.

Our source for the number of filings in the period 1914-34 was a table kindly provided to us by the Office of the Clerk of the Supreme Court. That table shows for each term the cases disposed of that term and the cases carried over to the next term. From these two figures it is possible to calculate the number of cases filed by solving the following equation for F_i (filings in the ith term), where D is the number of cases disposed of and C the number carried over: $C_{i-1} + F_i = D_i + C_i$. Although this method of computation should produce an accurate count of the number of cases filed each term, a comparison of the results of our computation with figures appearing in the report of the Freund study group for years in which the figures overlap indicates some minor discrepancies.

For the 1935-71 terms, our source was the study group's report. See Federal Judicial Center Report of the Study Group on the Case Load of the Supreme Court (Paul A. Freund, chairman), at A2 (Admin. Office U.S. Cts. for Fed. Jud. Center, Dec. 1972), for the study group's sources. For the 1972-74 terms our source was information supplied by the Office of the Clerk of the Supreme Court. The figures that we use for 1973 and 1974 were adjusted by the clerk to offset the distortion created by the fact that the 1973 term was an unusually long one. The unadjusted figures for the 1973 and 1974 terms are 4,187 and 3,417, respectively.

Caseload data presented in this monograph are based upon Supreme Court terms rather than calendar years, in order to be consistent with published statistics. Applications for review filed after the Court has adjourned for the summer, generally in June or July, are included in the statistics for the subsequent October term.

TABLE 1.1   Cases Filed in Supreme Court—1880-1974

Term	No.	Annual Rate of Change in 10-Year Moving Average (%)	Term	No.	Annual Rate of Change in 10-Year Moving Average (%)	Term	No.	Annual Rate of Change in 10-Year Moving Average (%)	Term	No.	Annual Rate of Change in 10-Year Moving Average (%)
1880	417	—	1904	403	+1.6	1928	776	+2.6	1952	1,283	+2.4
1881	411	—	1905	502	+3.0	1929	838	+3.5	1953	1,302	+2.4
1882	434	—	1906	484	+4.7	1930	845	+3.8	1954	1,397	+1.2
1883	439	—	1907	480	+4.1	1931	877	+2.7	1955	1,644	+2.5
1884	477	—	1908	494	−0.7	1932	897	+2.3	1956	1,802	+2.2
1885	493	—	1909	514	+3.0	1933	1,005	+4.7	1957	1,639	+2.5
1886	499	—	1910	516	+2.4	1934	937	+0.3	1958	1,819	+2.5
1887	489	—	1911	532	+3.2	1935	983	+2.3	1959	1,862	+4.1
1888	556	—	1912	521	+2.7	1936	950	+2.7	1960	1,940	+5.0
1889	500	—	1913	526	+2.0	1937	981	+2.6	1961	2,185	+6.0
1890	636	+4.6	1914	530	+2.6	1938	942	+1.8	1962	2,373	+6.5
1891	383	−0.6	1915	557	+1.1	1939	981	+1.5	1963	2,294	+5.5
1892	290	−2.9	1916	658	+3.4	1940	977	+1.4	1964	2,288	+4.7
1893	280	−3.3	1917	590	+2.1	1941	1,178	+5.1	1965	2,774	+5.7
1894	341	−3.0	1918	593	+1.8	1942	984	+0.9	1966	2,752	+4.5
1895	386	−2.4	1919	587	+1.3	1943	997	−0.1	1967	3,106	+6.7
1896	295	−4.7	1920	565	+0.9	1944	1,237	+3.0	1968	3,271	+6.2
1897	307	−4.4	1921	673	+2.5	1945	1,316	+3.3	1969	3,405	+6.2
1898	523	−0.8	1922	720	+3.4	1946	1,510	+5.3	1970	3,419	+5.6
1899	384	−2.9	1923	631	+1.8	1947	1,295	+2.8	1971	3,643	+5.2
1900	406	−6.0	1924	909	+6.2	1948	1,465	+4.6	1972	3,749	+4.7
1901	386	0.0	1925	790	+3.6	1949	1,270	+2.4	1973	3,943	+5.4
1902	391	+2.8	1926	718	+0.9	1950	1,181	+1.7	1974	3,661	+4.2
1903	430	+4.1	1927	751	+2.4	1951	1,234	+0.5			

Source: See note 2 *supra*.

4

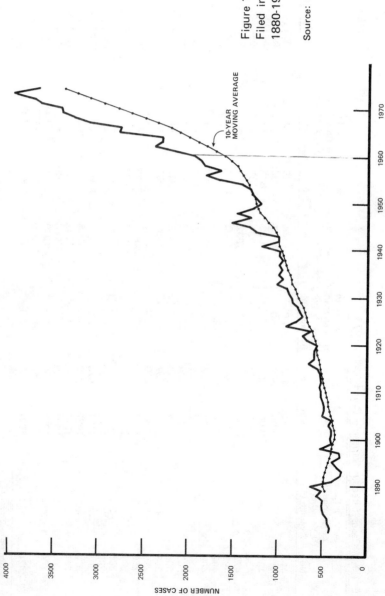

Figure 1. Increase in Cases Filed in Supreme Court—1880-1974

Source: Note 2 *supra*.

10-YEAR MOVING AVERAGE

NUMBER OF CASES

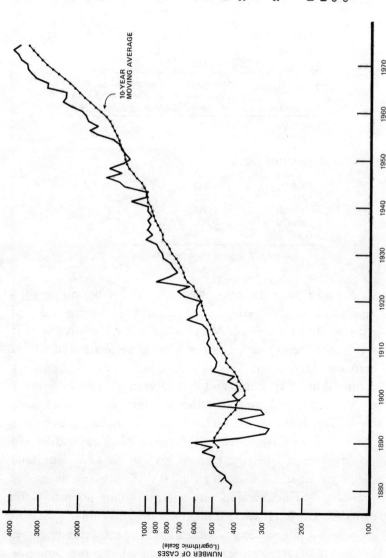

Figure 2. Proportionate
Increase in Cases Filed in
Supreme Court—1880-1974

Source: Note 2 *supra*.

N.B. Vertical distances measure
proportional, not absolute,
changes in the annual number
of cases filed with the Court.

10-YEAR
MOVING AVERAGE

NUMBER OF CASES
(Logarithmic Scale)

average. The picture that emerges shows the number of applications for review declining at an average annual rate of about 2 percent during the last decade of the nineteenth century, increasing steadily at an average annual rate of 2-3 percent throughout the first half of this century, and accelerating to more than 5 percent annually at about midcentury. The ten-year moving average has not yet been perceptibly deflected by the lower rates of growth since 1970,

TABLE 1.2
Average Increase in Number of Cases Filed
in Supreme Court—1880-1974

Decade	Average No. Cases Filed Annually	Average Annual Rate of Change in 10-Year Moving Average (%)
1880-89	472	-----
1890-99	383	−2.0
1900-09	449	+1.6
1910-19	561	+2.3
1920-29	737	+2.8
1930-39	940	+2.5
1940-49	1,223	+2.9
1950-59	1,516	+2.2
1960-69	2,639	+5.7
(1970-74) . . .	3,683	+5.0

Source: Computed from table 1.1.

which may or may not prove to be the beginning of a significant leveling off (or even decline) in the rate of growth of the caseload. Moreover, a constant (or, for that matter, declining) *rate* of growth could be associated with a dramatic increase in absolute numbers. This is seen in a comparison of figures 1 and 2. The vertical scale in figure 1 is arithmetic and measures the absolute numbers of cases filed. The logarithmic vertical scale in figure 2 measures proportionate differences in the numbers of cases filed and would show a constant rate of growth as a straight line. Although figure 2 indicates that the growth *rate* in recent years has not accelerated, the sharp absolute growth in the caseload explains why it is only recently that caseload growth—a phenomenon of many years' standing—has become a source of serious concern about the Supreme

Court's ability to discharge its duties. To illustrate: an increase of only 14 cases between 1907 and 1908 constituted a growth of 2.9 percent, whereas the same percentage growth between 1971 and 1972 required an increase of 106 cases.

Many people believe that the figures in table 1.1 in and of themselves demonstrate the existence of a crisis: if the Justices of the Supreme Court were not underemployed in 1935, when they had only 983 applications for review to pass on, how could they *not* be seriously overburdened in 1974, when that figure had risen to 3,661? And, assuming even the moderate annual rate of increase since 1969, the figure will be substantially larger in 1980, 1985, 1990, etc., so that even if the present caseload is supportable surely a point will soon be reached where everyone must agree that it is no longer so.

This is essentially the approach of the Freund study group and most of its successors. It reveals too casual an attitude toward statistical evidence. One should not simply *assume* that the Justices were working to full capacity at any time in the past; neither can their capacity be treated as fixed, when the number of supporting personnel, notably law clerks, can be and has been increased. Furthermore, a past trend, however long continued, should not be mechanically extrapolated into the indefinite future in the absence of a theory that explains the past trend and of evidence that the factors responsible for that trend will continue to exist in the future. Also, a simple aggregate of all of the applications for review filed each year, the basic statistical datum used by the Freund study group, may disguise important changes in the composition of the caseload that affect the actual *work*load of the Court and the likelihood that the caseload will continue to grow in the future at the same rate as in the past. A more probing inquiry into the statistical evidence relating to the increase in the Supreme Court's caseload is necessary before one can evaluate the drastic changes advocated by the Freund study group and by some of its successors.

The remainder of this monograph is organized as follows: Chapter 2 reviews the evolution of the Supreme Court's jurisdiction to its present state, the increase in its caseload, and the previous studies of its workload. Chapter 3 is a detailed statistical analysis of the caseload. It begins with a brief theoretical discussion of caseload change. This discussion is used to guide a statistical analysis that seeks to explain the growth of the Supreme Court's caseload over the past two decades by examining the composition of the caseload in terms of the subject matter of the cases filed and other factors that tend to be concealed by aggregate time series of the type presented in the report of the Freund study group. We believe that the key to understanding aggregate caseload growth lies in recognizing that growth patterns differ within the specific subject-matter categories that comprise the aggregate. The disaggregated statistics that we have gathered for the purposes of this study enable us to study these growth patterns. In the last part of chapter 3 we consider the likely rate of future growth in the Court's caseload.

Chapter 4 restates our findings with respect to the past and probable future growth of the caseload in terms of the actual workload of the Court and, consequently, its ability to discharge its responsibilities effectively. Our conclusion is that there is no statistical basis for a definite inference that the growth of the caseload has as yet substantially impaired that ability.

In chapter 5, finally, we consider how the jurisdiction or organization of the Supreme Court might be altered to alleviate whatever workload pressures are deemed already excessive or likely soon to become so. We discuss the actual proposals that have been placed on the table and a number of other possibilities, mainly of a housekeeping rather than of a jurisdictional character, that seem worthy of consideration although they have not been in the forefront of the public debate. These include greater delegation to individual Justices of the screening of applications for review, dividing the Court into panels for the consideration and decision of certain kinds of cases, and the adoption by the Court of clear-cut guidelines for the grant and denial of applications for review. We conclude that although there may be, or may soon develop, a Supreme Court workload problem, the actual or imminent problem does not represent a crisis requiring or justifying the creation of a new national court, which is the usual solution suggested.

CHAPTER 2
HISTORICAL OVERVIEW

A. The Caseload of the Supreme Court in Its Early Years

The workload of the Justices of the United States Supreme Court has been a matter of controversy almost since the first term of court in 1790. But until the late nineteenth century, the main problem was not the *caseload* of the Court but the burdens imposed on the Justices by their circuit duties (discussed in the next part of this chapter). Notwithstanding the historical importance of its early landmark decisions, the Supreme Court sat infrequently and for short periods of time.

The Judiciary Act of 1789[1] had conferred on the Supreme Court appellate jurisdiction over final judgments of the circuit courts where the amount in controversy exceeded $2,000. The circuit courts, also created by the 1789 act, had some appellate jurisdiction over the district courts but were primarily trial courts, mostly for diversity litigation,[2] while in this early period the district courts were mainly concerned with admiralty cases. The Supreme Court was also given appellate jurisdiction over final judgments of the highest court of a state when certain questions involving the validity or construction of federal law were in issue. Until the end of the nineteenth century there was virtually no Supreme Court review of criminal cases.[3]

Between 1790 and 1801 the appellate jurisdiction of the Supreme Court was invoked in only 87 cases, 80 of them federal.[4] Of the 80 cases, 36 were based on diversity,

---

1. Act of Sept. 24, 1789, ch. 20, 1 Stat. 73.
2. That is, litigation over which the federal courts have jurisdiction only by virtue of the fact that the litigants are citizens of different states.
3. An 1802 statute (Act of Apr. 29, 1802, ch. 31, 2 Stat. 156) provided that federal criminal cases would be reviewed by the Supreme Court if there was a division of opinion in the circuit court, but only the disputed question was certified to the Supreme Court. This system lasted until 1889, when Supreme Court review of federal capital cases was provided for by statute. Act of Feb. 6, 1889, ch. 113, 25 Stat. 655.
4. Julius Goebel, Jr., History of the Supreme Court of the United States: Vol. 1, Antecedents and Beginnings to 1801, at 802-13 (New York: Macmillan Co., 1971).

35 were admiralty cases, and 9 were civil actions brought by the United States. Of the 79 cases disposed of by the Court during this period, 53 involved either a federal statute or the Constitution. President Jefferson reported that during the same period a total of 8,358 cases had been instituted in the circuit courts.[5]

Although the business of the Supreme Court increased substantially in subsequent decades, the overall caseload remained small until after the Civil War, as shown in table 2.1.[6] However, in evaluating the figures in this table, one should bear in mind that most of these cases were within the obligatory jurisdiction of the court; the discretionary (certiorari) jurisdiction did not become of great significance until the twentieth century.

TABLE 2.1
Cases on Supreme Court Docket, Selected Terms—1810-1970

Term	No.	Term	No.	Term	No.
1810 . . .	98	1870 . . .	636	1930 . . .	1,039
1820 . . .	137	1880 . . .	1,212	1940 . . .	1,109
1830 . . .	143	1890 . . .	1,816	1950 . . .	1,335
1840 . . .	92	1900 . . .	723	1960 . . .	2,313
1850 . . .	253	1910 . . .	1,116	1970 . . .	4,212
1860 . . .	310	1920 . . .	975		

Source: *1810-1920:* Congressional reports; Frankfurter & Landis, *supra* note 5. *1930-70:* Office of the Clerk, U.S. Supreme Court.

Among other contrasts with the present-day Court, the Supreme Court of the nineteenth century was primarily a private-law court, as shown in table 2.2; and Supreme Court terms were short. The system of two terms a year that had prevailed since the adoption of the Judiciary Act of 1789 was abolished, apparently for political reasons,[7] in

5. See Felix Frankfurter & James M. Landis, The Business of the Supreme Court: A Study in the Federal Judicial System 13 (New York: Macmillan Co., 1928). The reliability of these figures is questioned in Goebel, *supra* note 4, at 569-73.

6. It should be noted that the figures in table 2.1 refer to total cases on docket, not filings. Hence the discrepancies between these figures and those in table 1.1.

7. See Richard E. Ellis, The Jeffersonian Crisis: Courts and Politics in the Young Republic 59 (New York: Oxford University Press, 1971).

TABLE 2.2
Subject Matter of Supreme Court Dispositions by
Written Opinion—1825 and 1875

Subject-Matter Categories	No. Opinions	
	1825 Term	1875 Term
Bill of Rights	0	2
Slave trade	3	0
International law, war and peace	2	5
Interstate commerce	0	2
Land legislation	0	11
Construction of miscellaneous statutes .	4	16
Admiralty	2	5
Bankruptcy	0	13
Patents and trademarks	1	8
Contract suits against government	0	12
Common law topics	10	81
Jurisdiction and procedure	4	30
All others	0	8
Total	26	193

Source: Frankfurter & Landis, *supra* note 5, at 302.

1802, and beginning with the February term 1803 the Court met only once a year, and then for less than two months.[8] The length of the term was gradually and irregularly extended,[9] as shown in table 2.3, by moving the start of the term back to January and eventually to December.

TABLE 2.3
Length of Terms and Flow of Cases on
Supreme Court Docket—1825-45

Term	Days	Number of Cases		
		On Docket	Disposed Of	Left
1825 . . .	43	164	38	126
1830 . . .	70	143	73	71
1835 . . .	64	89	41	48
1840 . . .	55	92	58	34
1845 . . .	99	177	53	120

Source: Cong. Globe, 30th Cong., 1st Sess., Appendix 351 (1848).

---

8. Act of Apr. 29, 1802, ch. 31, 2 Stat. 156. See Carl B. Swisher, History of the Supreme Court of the United States: Vol. 5, The Taney Period 1836—64, at 275 (New York: Macmillan Publishing Co., 1974).

9. See Act of May 4, 1826, ch. 37, 4 Stat. 160; Act of June 17, 1844, ch. 96, 5 Stat. 676; S. Doc. No. 91, 29th Cong., 1st Sess. (1846); Swisher, *supra* note 8, at 284, 291.

The modern system of long terms that begin in October can be traced back to 1869, when the Court adjourned its December 1868 term to October 1869, thus providing itself with two extra months of the December 1868 term before the opening of the December term 1869. This device was employed until, in 1873, Congress fixed the beginning of Court terms in October.[10] From then on, the terms of the Court lasted from October through late spring (the first half of May for the remainder of the century).[11]

B.   The Circuit Duties of Supreme Court Justices

In the early years, the Justices had a serious workload problem as a result of the decision of the first Congress to man the circuit courts with district judges plus the Justices of the Supreme Court. Under this system "three tiers of courts were operated by two sets of judges."[12] (See table 2.4.) The Justices began complaining about their duty to ride circuit soon after the establishment of the Court. In 1792 they wrote to President Washington objecting to the

TABLE 2.4
Changes in the Composition of the Circuit Courts—1789-1869

Year	No. Circuits	No. Judges Required for Circuit Court	Statutory Size of Supreme Court
1789	3	1 dist. judge and 2 justices	6
1793	3	1 dist. judge and 1 justice	6
1802a	6		6
1807	7		7
1837	9	1 dist. judge *or* 1 justice	9
1855b . . .	10	*or*, after 1869,	9
1866	9	1 circuit judge	7
1869c	9		9

aThe short-lived changes caused by the Second Judiciary Act of 1801 are ignored.

bA separate circuit judge who was not a Supreme Court Justice was provided for the new California circuit.

cNine separate circuit judgeships were authorized.

10. Act of Jan. 24, 1873, ch. 64, 17 Stat. 419.
11. Charles Fairman, History of the Supreme Court of the United States: Vol. 6, Reconstruction and Reunion 1864-88, Part One, at 69 (New York: Macmillan Co., 1971).
12. Frankfurter & Landis, *supra* note 5, at 14.

excessive burdens placed upon them as a result of having to hold 27 circuit courts a year from New Hampshire to Georgia in the most severe seasons of the year, in addition to two sessions of the Supreme Court at Philadelphia.[13] They also noted the peculiarity that, as Supreme Court Justices, they had to review the errors they might have committed in their capacity as circuit judges. Given "the dangers and miseries of overturned vehicles, runaway horses, rivers in full flood, or icebound and scruffy taverns,"[14] their letter understated their case. But the only relief Congress would grant was to dispense with the requirement that two Justices be present at every circuit court.[15]

An act of the lame-duck Federalist Congress in 1801 creating 16 separate circuit court judgeships became entangled in partisan politics and was promptly repealed.[16] The Jeffersonians who succeeded the Federalists required two annual sessions of the circuit courts (organized into six circuits) in each of the then 17 districts. But whereas before the abortive Federalist reform effort the circuit courts had been composed of one district judge and one Supreme Court Justice, now only a single judge or Justice was required for holding the circuit court.

As the country expanded westward, the circuit-riding system became progressively more unworkable, even bizarre. In the spring of 1838 the caseload of the circuit courts, not counting the district courts exercising circuit court functions, comprised approximately 6,000 cases.[17] To be sure, roughly 4,700 of these cases had accumulated in Alabama, Louisiana, and Mississippi due to the creation of two new circuits in 1837, but the number of cases (unevenly) distributed across the remaining circuits was still

---

13. Goebel, *supra* note 4, at 565.
14. *Id.* at 569.
15. Act of Mar. 2, 1793, ch. 22, 1 Stat. 333.
16. Act of Feb. 13, 1801, ch. 4, 2 Stat. 89; see Ellis, *supra* note 7, at 36-52.
17. S. Doc. No. 50, 25th Cong., 3d Sess. (1839).

very considerable in comparison to the 85 cases on the docket of the Supreme Court during its 1838 term. New territories and states in the West were without circuit courts; and with the caseload and terms of the Supreme Court expanding, many circuit courts were increasingly manned by the district judges alone. These district judges frequently sat in sole judgment, on appeal, over their own district court decisions—while one Supreme Court Justice reportedly traveled 10,000 miles on circuit duty in 1838 (see table 2.5).

TABLE 2.5
Miles Traveled by Justices on Circuit Duty—1838

Justice	Miles	Circuit	States in Circuit
Taney	458	Fourth	Del., Md.
Barbour	1,498	Fifth	Va., N.C.
Story	1,896	First	Mass., Me., N.H., R.I.
Baldwin	2,000	Third	Pa., N.J.
Wayne	2,370	Sixth	S.C., Ga.
McLean	2,500	Seventh	Ill., Ohio, Ind., Mich.
Thompson . . .	2,590	Second	N.Y., Conn., Vt.
Catron	3,464	Eighth	Tenn., Ky., Mo.
McKinley	10,000	Ninth	Ala., La., Miss., Ark.

Source: Frankfurter & Landis, *supra* note 5, at 49; S. Doc. No. 50, 25th Cong., 3d Sess. (1839).

When the caseload of the Supreme Court began to increase rapidly after the Civil War (see table 2.1), Congress finally provided some relief from circuit riding. The Act of 1869 provided for the appointment of nine separate circuit judges with the same authority as possessed by the circuit Justices. Although the act did not abolish the circuit duties of Supreme Court Justices, it required their attendance at only one term of the circuit court in each district of their circuit, every two years.[18] But in practice the press of circuit business continued to require more frequent attendance.[19]

---

18. Act of Apr. 10, 1869, ch. 22, 16 Stat. 44.
19. Fairman, *supra* note 11, at 560. The circuit courts were finally abolished in 1911. See note 30 *infra* and accompanying text.

C.   The Supreme Court's Caseload from the Civil War to the Judiciary Act of 1925

The dramatic increases in the Supreme Court's caseload after the Civil War were caused partly by a rising volume of diversity litigation, partly by litigation arising from the Reconstruction amendments and legislation (although these enactments did not have a major impact on the caseload until the end of the century, when the Supreme Court began to apply the Fourteenth Amendment to state regulation of the economy), but mostly by legislation enlarging the Court's jurisdiction. The Act of March 3, 1875, conferred on the federal courts for the first time a general federal-question jurisdiction, extending to all civil suits in which the amount in controversy exceeded $500 and which arose under the Constitution, laws, or treaties of the United States.[20] Although this reform was coupled with an increase in the jurisdictional minimum for Supreme Court review to $5,000 in cases coming from the circuit courts,[21] the insufficiency of this limitation is suggested by an unsuccessful attempt only one year later to increase the minimum to $10,000.[22]

In 1889 Congress provided for the first time for review of convictions in capital cases,[23] and in 1891 this was expanded to all cases of "infamous crimes,"[24] which the Court interpreted to mean all cases in which the accused might be sentenced to imprisonment even if the punishment actually imposed was only a fine.[25] The result was an immediate and dramatic increase in criminal appeals.

The Supreme Court itself contributed to the rise in its caseload. Beginning with *Gelpcke v. Dubuque*,[26] the Court

---

20. Act of Mar. 3, 1875, ch. 137, 18 Stat. 470.
21. Act of Feb. 16, 1875, ch. 77, 18 Stat. 315.
22. See Frankfurter & Landis, *supra* note 5, at 79.
23. Act of Feb. 6, 1889, ch. 113, 25 Stat. 655.
24. Act of Mar. 3, 1891, ch. 517, 26 Stat. 826.
25. *In re* Claasen, 140 U.S. 200 (1891); see Frankfurter & Landis, *supra* note 5, at 109-13.
26. 68 U.S. (1 Wall.) 175 (1863).

between 1863 and 1888 decided some 200 cases on rail-road bonds. Relying on the notion of federal common law,[27] the Court not only reversed state court decisions that "judicially repudiated" contracts authorized under previous state decisions but, as Fairman explains, went much further—"enforcing bonds which the State court had held invalid without overruling any decision; construing State statutes—on the powers of municipal officers, on debt limits, on the privilege of railroad corporations, etc.,— contrary to the construction given them by the State courts. . . ."[28]

When, by 1890, the caseload of the Supreme Court had reached 1,800 cases (see table 2.1), it was clear that a drastic remedy was necessary; and 90 years after the failure of the Federalists to achieve it, Congress, by the Act of March 3, 1891, finally provided for a separate set of circuit courts of appeals.[29] Even so, the old circuit courts were not abolished (this did not occur until 1911),[30] and the new circuit courts of appeals were, in theory, to be composed of two circuit judges and one Supreme Court Justice for whom, however, a district judge could be substituted. The substantial impact of the act on the Supreme Court's caseload is reflected in tables 1.1 and 2.1.

Due to the considerable expansion in federal legislative activity around the turn of the century, including such caseload-generating items as employers' liability legislation, the relief afforded by the 1891 act was only temporary. Furthermore, the Court itself fostered litigation by its propensity to declare social and economic legislation unconstitutional:

> In the thirty four year period between the Judiciary Acts of 1891 and 1925 the Court invalidated 30 federal, 205 state, and

---

27. Which had originated in the famous case of Swift v. Tyson, 41 U.S. (16 Pet.) 1 (1842).

28. Fairman, *supra* note 11, at 919; see also Harold M. Hyman, A More Perfect Union: The Impact of the Civil War and Reconstruction on the Constitution 230 (New York: Alfred A. Knopf, 1973).

29. Act of Mar. 3, 1891, ch. 517, 26 Stat. 826.

30. Act of Mar. 3, 1911, ch. 231, 36 Stat. 1087.

35 municipal statutes. Contrast this with the one-hundred and two year period between 1789 and 1891 when 20 federal, 138 state and 9 municipal laws fell. In 1925, when Taft complained that the Court was approximately two years behind in its docket, his Court had managed, in a space of three years, to find 4 federal, 36 state and three municipal laws unconstitutional.[31]

An important contemporary development was Congress's increasing emphasis on the discretionary (certiorari) jurisdiction of the Supreme Court. In 1914 Congress provided for Supreme Court review, by writ of certiorari, of state court decisions in favor of rights claimed under federal law.[32] Previously only state court decisions *denying* a federal right had been reviewable. In 1916 Congress curtailed the Court's obligatory (*i.e.,* writ of error) jurisdiction in the latter class of cases (*i.e.,* cases where the state court decision was adverse to the claimant of federal rights) by confining it to cases where the state court decision was either against the validity of federal law or authority or in favor of the validity of a state law challenged as inconsistent with federal law, and providing that in other cases the exclusive mode of Supreme Court review was the discretionary writ of certiorari.[33] Thus the Court's jurisdiction was enlarged, and its docket rose (*e.g.,* from 723 cases in the 1900 term to 1,093 in the 1915 term), but an increasing fraction of the docket consisted of cases that the Court was authorized to refuse to review on the merits.

D.   The Judiciary Act of 1925 and After

The last major effort to reduce the Court's workload was made when, at the urging of the Court, Congress passed the Judiciary Act of 1925.[34] A principal purpose of

---

31. Paper by Mary Cornelia Porter, Politics, Ideology and the Workload of the Supreme Court: Some Historical Perspectives 7 (prepared for presentation at the annual meeting of the Midwest Political Science Ass'n, May 1-3, 1975, Chicago).
32. Act of Dec. 23, 1914, ch. 2, 38 Stat. 790.
33. Act of Sept. 6, 1916, ch. 448, 39 Stat. 726.
34. Act of Feb. 13, 1925, ch. 229, 43 Stat. 93.

the act was to lessen what was considered an excessive
burden by further limiting the Court's obligatory jurisdiction. Frankfurter and Landis, in their evaluation of the
act,[35] understated its impact by failing to count denied
and dismissed petitions for certiorari. Table 2.6 repairs this
omission and reveals that the 1925 act did indeed reduce
substantially the number of cases that the Court was obli-
gated to review on the merits.[36]

TABLE 2.6
Cases Arising Within Supreme Court's Obligatory
and Discretionary Jurisdictions—1923-30

Term	Cases Filed	Percent Obligatory	Percent Discretionary
1923 . . .	637	39	61
1924 . . .	724	40	60
1925 . . .	781	36	64
1926 . . .	817	32	68
1927 . . .	812	20	80
1928 . . .	788	19	81
1929 . . .	778	14	86
1930 . . .	874	15	85

Source: Felix Frankfurter & James M. Landis, The
Supreme Court Under the Judiciary Act of 1925, 42
Harv. L. Rev. 1 (1928); Felix Frankfurter & James M.
Landis, The Business of the Supreme Court at October
Term, 1928, 43 Harv. L. Rev. 33 (1929); *id.*, 1929, 44
Harv. L. Rev. 1 (1930); *id.,* 1930, 45 Harv. L. Rev.
271 (1931).

Frankfurter and Landis concluded that because of the
steady increase in the number of petitions for certiorari,
shifting cases from the obligatory to the discretionary jurisdiction of the Court could not be the final answer to the
workload problem,[37] and in this they were correct: petitions for certiorari now make up more than 90 percent of
the entire docket.[38] Most students of the workload prob-

---

35. See sources to table 2.6 *infra.*
36. Notice that the figures in table 2.6 for cases filed differ, sometimes
quite significantly, from the data provided us by the Clerk of the Court and
used in table 1.1. This discrepancy undermines our confidence in the percentages revealed in table 2.6—but the sources used in this table are the only
available sources known to us for computing these percentages.
37. See Frankfurter & Landis, *supra* note 5, at 256.
38. Federal Judicial Center Report of the Study Group on the Case Load
of the Supreme Court (Paul A. Freund, chairman), at A8 (Admin. Office U.S.
Cts. for Fed. Jud. Center, Dec. 1972) [hereinafter cited as Freund report].

lem have recommended that the remaining obligatory appellate jurisdiction be eliminated, and we concur, but it must be recognized that making the Court's entire appellate jurisdiction discretionary will not, at this stage, reduce the Court's workload substantially, since there is no longer any significant difference in the Court's treatment of appeals and of certiorari petitions.

The data collected by Frankfurter and Landis persuaded them that by 1925 the Supreme Court had ceased to be a "common law court."[39] They accurately foresaw that the Court would one day be primarily a constitutional court. Table 2.7 presents data on the composition of the Court's caseload that provide a baseline for our statistics in the next chapter.

TABLE 2.7
Subject Matter of Certiorari Petitions—1929-30 Terms Compared to 1937-38 Terms

Major Categories	1929-30		1937-38	
	No.	% of Total	No.	% of Total
Constitutional law	121	9	232	14
Bill of Rights	9	---	12	---
Commerce Clause	0	---	20	---
Due process	103	---	147	---
Full faith and credit	4	---	9	---
Impairment of contract	5	---	13	---
Other	0	---	31	---
Statutory regulation under the Commerce Clause	127	9	88	5
Federal tax	314	22	259	15
Common law	230	16	238	14
Bankruptcy	61	4	144	9
Patents	66	5	108	6
All others	499	35	610	37
Total	1,418	100	1,679	100

Source: Felix Frankfurter & James M. Landis, The Business of the Supreme Court at October Term, 1929, 44 Harv. L. Rev. 1 (1930); *id.*, 1930, 45 Harv. L. Rev. 271 (1931); Henry M. Hart, Jr., The Business of the Supreme Court at the October Terms, 1937 and 1938, 53 Harv. L. Rev. 579 (1940).

39. Frankfurter & Landis, *supra* note 5, at 307.

E.　Previous Efforts to Determine the Workload
　　Implications of Caseload Increase

The shift to a jurisdiction that is almost completely discretionary has made it difficult to determine the true gravity of the Court's workload problem. There have, however, been sporadic efforts to answer this question. For example, Harper and his associates analyzed all denied certiorari petitions on the appellate docket in the 1949-1951 terms. They calculated that in the 1949 term, for example, the Court had denied certiorari in 61 cases where, in their opinion, it should have been granted. They concluded that the Court was overworked and made suggestions for regulating the flow of cases other than by discretion.[40] But they neglected to investigate the question whether the Court was granting certiorari in cases where it should have been denying certiorari. If the number of cases in which certiorari was improperly denied equalled the number in which certiorari was improperly granted, that would suggest that the Court's problem was one not of excessive workload but of inept screening.

A direct attempt to measure the Supreme Court's workload was made by Hart in 1959.[41] The results of his analysis are summarized in table 2.8. The analysis raises many questions. Were Hart's estimates regarding the actual allocation of time by the Justices realistic? If so, is such an allocation of time desirable, or should more time be allocated to initial review or to opinion writing or to some other task? If more time were available for opinion writing, would it actually be used for that purpose? While Hart found the overall caseload formidable, his own remedy was

---

40. Fowler V. Harper & Alan S. Rosenthal, What the Supreme Court Did Not Do in the 1949 Term—An Appraisal of Certiorari, 99 U. Pa. L. Rev. 293 (1950); Fowler V. Harper & Edwin D. Etherington, What the Supreme Court Did Not Do During the 1950 Term, 100 U. Pa. L. Rev. 354 (1951); Fowler V. Harper & George C. Pratt, What the Supreme Court Did Not Do During the 1951 Term, 101 U. Pa. L. Rev. 439 (1953).

41. Henry M. Hart, Jr., The Supreme Court, 1958 Term: The Time Chart of the Justices, 73 Harv. L. Rev. 84 (1959).

not to reduce the inflow of cases; rather, he urged the Court to accept, and decide, fewer cases. "Regretfully and with deference, it has to be said that too many of the Court's opinions are about what one would expect would be written in twenty-four hours."[42] He warned "with all possible gravity" that the Court's qualitative failure threatened to undermine professional respect.[43]

TABLE 2.8
Hart's Time Chart

Work Category	No. Hours	%
Initial review of 1,400 petitions and appeals[a] . . .	242	14
Oral Argument (125 cases)	240	14
24 conferences	132	8
Study of briefs and records in 125 argued cases . .	250	14
Opinion writing (22 for each Justice)	528	31
Studying opinions of colleagues (176 opinions) . .	140	8
Miscellaneous judicial work	196	11
Total	1,728[b]	100

Source: Hart, *supra* note 41.

[a]This number was arrived at after adjusting for an arithmetical error made by Hart and after deducting cases that Hart allotted to the summer recess (see note b *infra*).

[b]The total of 1,728 available hours assumes a term of 36 weeks, each comprising six eight-hour days. Hart treated the 16 weeks of summer recess separately. Assumptions about caseload are based on averages derived from the 1953-57 terms.

Justice Douglas answered Hart with his own statistics.[44] These emphasized the steep increase (see table 2.9) in petitions for certiorari in forma pauperis (*i.e.*, by indigents),

TABLE 2.9
Increase in Indigent as Compared to
Paid Certiorari Petitions—1938-58

Term	In Forma Pauperis Petitions	Paid Petitions
1938	85	857
1948	447	773
1958	772	886

Source: Douglas, *supra* note 44.

42. *Id.* at 100.
43. *Id.* at 101.
44. William O. Douglas, The Supreme Court and Its Case Load, 45 Cornell L.Q. 401 (1960).

which, he asserted, while increasing the caseload did not substantially increase the Court's workload because most of the indigent claims were frivolous. The Justice contended that most of the things Hart had asked for were already being done: "We have fewer oral arguments than we once had, fewer opinions to write, and shorter weeks to work. I do not recall any time in my twenty years or more of service on the Court when we had more time for research, deliberation, debate and meditation."[45]

The Supreme Court's caseload is now almost twice what it was when Justice Douglas responded to Professor Hart. The fact that the number of cases that the Court decides with full opinion has remained approximately constant over this period—with the result that the percentage of certiorari petitions granted has declined by about a half—has, for most observers, turned Hart's question whether the Court was deciding too many cases into the question whether the Court is deciding too few.

With this difference, the Freund study group in 1972 reached conclusions similar to those of Hart:

> The statistics of the Court's current workload, both in absolute terms and in the mounting trend, are impressive evidence that the conditions essential for the performance of the Court's mission do not exist. . . .
> Over the past thirty-five years . . . the number of cases filed has grown about fourfold, while the number of cases in which the Court has heard oral argument before decision has remained substantially constant. Two consequences can be inferred. Issues that would have been decided on the merits a generation ago are passed over by the Court today; and second, the consideration given to the cases actually decided on the merits is compromised by the pressures of "processing" the inflated docket of petitions and appeals.[46]

In analyzing the debate that has followed the release of the Freund study group's report,[47] one is not always certain whether critics of the report disagree with its diag-

45. *Id.* at 411.
46. Freund report, *supra* note 38, at 5-6.
47. See references in note 2, *supra* p. xi.

nosis, or with its proposed cure (a national court of appeals, mainly to screen out unmeritorious certiorari petitions), or with both. Justice Brennan, who among the Justices responded in greatest detail, criticized the diagnosis in a revealing paper not very different from Justice Douglas's response to Hart.[48] He also disagreed with the Freund group's suggested remedy. Some sitting and former Justices are on record as agreeing with Justice Brennan, while others are known to share Chief Justice Burger's desire for measures to reduce the Court's workload. As we shall see in chapter 5, proposals for alleviating the alleged workload problem have mushroomed since the publication of the Freund study group's report. What has thus become a perennial debate over the implications of a rising Supreme Court caseload cannot be resolved intelligently on the basis of the kinds of quantitative and qualitative evidence thus far advanced. The problem requires a fuller theoretical and empirical analysis. The next two chapters attempt such an analysis.

---

48. William J. Brennan, Jr., The National Court of Appeals: Another Dissent, 40 U. Chi. L. Rev. 473 (1973).

CHAPTER 3
NATURE AND CAUSES OF THE RISE OF THE COURT'S CASELOAD

A.   A Theory of Supreme Court Caseload Change

A striking characteristic of previous studies of the Supreme Court's caseload, with the exception of Frankfurter and Landis's classic, is that they do not inquire deeply into the reasons for the secular growth in the Court's caseload. Rather they assume that this growth is the product of factors wholly external to the legal system that guarantee continued growth regardless of any legal reforms. The assumption is typified in the statement of the Freund study group that "the lesson of history teaches that, independent of other factors, the number of cases will continue to increase as population grows and the economy expands."[1] When these words were written, few people expected either population or economic growth to cease, and thus it followed in the minds of the writers that continued growth in the caseload must be the premise of any proposal to alleviate the Supreme Court's workload pressures.

This approach assumes away several major issues. The first is whether the caseload will in fact continue to grow (and if so at what rate), even assuming that population and the economy continue to grow. The second is whether caseload growth is indeed a function solely of factors external to the legal system rather than, at least in part, of the law and its administration. What is needed, and attempted here, is a theory of the demand for Supreme Court review.

The applications for review filed with the Supreme

---

1. Federal Judicial Center Report of the Study Group on the Case Load of the Supreme Court (Paul A. Freund, chairman), at 3 (Admin. Office U.S. Cts. for Fed. Jud. Center, Dec. 1972) [hereinafter cited as Freund report].

Court represent the apex of a pyramid, illustrated below for the federal tax area:

Civil cases decided by Supreme Court	4
Civil cases decided by courts of appeals	363
Civil cases docketed in trial courts	9,932
Civil cases received by appellate division (of the Internal Revenue Service)	18,569
Returns examined	2,030,655
Federal tax returns filed	121,609,260

Source: H. Todd Miller, Comment: A Court of Tax Appeals Revisited, 85 Yale L.J. 228, 233 (1975) (1974 data).

The base of the pyramid consists of the myriad transactions and events that give rise to potentially litigable disputes ("primary behavior"). Some fraction of the disputes generated by primary behavior are litigated, and some of these litigated disputes are either litigated in federal district courts or, if litigated in state courts, nonetheless involve issues of federal law. Some fraction of the decisions in such cases are appealed—to a federal court of appeals if the case was brought in a federal district court (or arose before a federal administrative agency) and to a state supreme court if the case was brought in a state trial court—and, in turn, some fraction of the decisions of the federal courts of appeals and state supreme courts (in federal cases) are appealed to the Supreme Court. Clearly, then, any factor that affects either the amount of primary behavior or the fraction of the disputes arising from that behavior that survives each of the stages from an initial dispute to seeking Supreme Court review can affect the number of applications for review filed in the Supreme Court.[2]

Consider primary behavior—the transactions and events that can give rise to a legal dispute or controversy, such as strikes, loans, acts of violence, government contracts, and highway accidents. Although these events are clearly affected by factors (largely) external to the legal system,

---

2. Often, of course, with a considerable time lag, because of the time it takes for a legal dispute to proceed through the various stages of the litigation-appeal process before it reaches the Supreme Court.

such as population and economic growth, they may also be affected by legislation and other legal phenomena, including judicial decisions. For example, state or federal legislation dealing with criminal law may affect the incidence of "crime" by altering the definition of what is criminally punishable. So also may decisions by the Supreme Court relating to the power of the states to declare conduct criminal. Indirect effects are also possible: decisions affecting prison conditions, punishment, procedural rights, etc., could affect the crime rate by altering the incentives of people to commit crimes. All of these factors are internal, not external, to the legal system.

How much of the underlying, or primary, behavior will give rise to litigation is influenced by a variety of other factors, including the relative costs of litigation and of settlement, the uncertainty of the law (which increases the difficulty of arriving at a mutually attractive settlement by complicating the prediction of the outcome of litigation), and the stakes in the case (which magnify any differences between the parties with respect to the settlement terms, relative to the costs of litigation).[3] Among the parameters that affect these determinants of the litigation rate, one of particular importance to our study is the amount of previous litigation in an area. The greater the accumulation of precedents as a result of earlier appellate decisions, the less uncertainty one can expect with respect to the rules of law; and greater certainty should reduce the litigation rate both directly by encouraging settlements and indirectly by guiding the primary behavior that might give rise to legal disputes in the first place. Thus it is simplistic to forecast a perpetual, monotonic increase in the litigation rate solely on the basis of the fact that the underlying primary activity is expected to grow monotonically.

---

3. See, *e.g.,* William M. Landes, An Economic Analysis of the Courts, in Gary S. Becker & William M. Landes, eds., Essays in the Economics of Crime and Punishment 164 (New York: National Bureau of Economic Research, 1974); Richard A. Posner, An Economic Approach to Legal Procedure and Judicial Administration, 2 J. Leg. Studies 399, 422-26 (1973).

Figure 3 illustrates the more complex time pattern of litigation that can be expected to result from initially high levels of litigation which lead eventually to a reduction in the litigation rate through the accumulation of precedents. Figure 3 assumes a new activity. The initial level of litigation is high due to the uncertainty of the law applicable to a new activity and rises rapidly as the increase in the underlying activity generates numerous disputes. But, by increasing the number of precedents that offer guidance to the resolution of these disputes and that also reduce the incidence of such disputes by structuring the underlying activity, the high and rising level of litigation eventually reinforces the effect of time on the accumulation of precedents, and uncertainty is reduced, leading to a decline in the volume of litigation, a decline due to both a rise in the settlement rate and the avoidance of primary activities giving rise to legal disputes.[4]

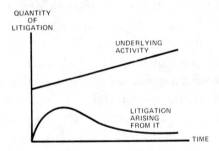

Figure 3. The Time Pattern of Litigation

Since the jurisdiction of the Supreme Court does not extend to all lawsuits but only to cases within the federal appellate jurisdiction, the demand for Supreme Court review is also affected by a multitude of special factors affecting the exercise of that jurisdiction, including the relative attractiveness of federal versus state trial courts in matters within the diversity jurisdiction of the federal courts, the definition of federal rights by Congress and the

---

4. See William M. Landes & Richard A. Posner, Legal Precedent: A Theoretical and Empirical Analysis (J. Law & Econ., in press); Spencer L. Kimball, The Role of the Court in the Development of Insurance Law, 1957 Wis. L. Rev. 520, 521-22, 562.

Supreme Court, and changes in the incremental costs of appealing from an adverse trial court judgment. A frequently overlooked point is the extent to which the Supreme Court itself controls the demand for its services through its power to recognize a new, or extinguish a recognized, federal statutory or constitutional right by interpreting or reinterpreting a federal statute or constitutional provision.

Only a fraction of the appellate cases within the federal jurisdiction show up in the caseload of the Supreme Court, for not all losing parties in the appellate courts seek to invoke the jurisdiction of the Court. A potentially important factor affecting the incentive to seek Supreme Court review and thus the percentage of appellate cases that are brought before the Court is the probability that review will be granted. We conjecture that caseload increases, both generally and in the Supreme Court, are eventually self-limiting. Changes in caseload affect the value of a court to the litigants and hence their demand for its services. If the caseload of a court increases faster than its ability to process cases, the court will respond either by increasing the waiting period for litigants or by reducing the fraction of cases that it accepts for review. The former has been the usual response of courts—most courts are not empowered to refuse to review cases within their jurisdiction. The Supreme Court has the power to refuse review and has used it, rather than delay, to prevent an imbalance between the demand for and the supply of its services. Whether delay or refusal to review is used to ration access to the court, the value of the court's services to the applicant for review is reduced.[5] Other things being equal, this should reduce the number of applications filed. Conversely, if a court shortens the queue or accepts an increasing number of cases, the

---

5. Actually the analysis of delay is more complex. Some petitions for certiorari are filed solely for the purpose of delaying the entry of a final judgment adverse to the petitioner. The longer the Court delays in acting on (i.e., denying) the petition, the more valuable to this class of applicants will filing petitions be. However, there is no indication of a substantial secular increase in Supreme Court delay in the disposition of applications for review. Cf. table 4.3.

value of review will rise and this should induce an increase in the number of cases filed.

In view of the complexity of the interactions that determine caseload changes over time and the lack of data with respect to many of the important variables, we have not attempted to construct a complete, empirically testable model of caseload change. For our purposes, it will be sufficient, by identifying and (in the next part of this chapter) verifying the empirical significance of some of the factors relevant to caseload change, to dispel the simplistic impression that caseload changes are caused solely by broad social trends external to the legal system.

B.   Empirical Analysis of the Caseload Increase

1.   Study Method

In order to understand how the factors discussed in the previous part have in fact affected the Supreme Court's caseload, it is necessary to disaggregate the caseload figures presented in chapter 1 into categories defined by subject matter, type of litigant, etc. Our disaggregated study begins with the 1956 term of the Court—an arbitrary starting point chosen because of the limitations of our resources rather than for any theoretical reason, but one that allows us to study the caseload over a period during which it more than doubled. The most recent term included in the study is 1973.

Our study methods were different for the two dockets that comprise the bulk of the caseload.[6] The "appellate docket" consists of those applications for review (whether petitions for certiorari or appeals) in which the applicant submits a printed petition for certiorari (or its counterpart in appeal cases, a "jurisdictional statement") in accordance

---

6. We have excluded from our tabulations and analysis the very small number of cases in which the original rather than appellate jurisdiction of the Supreme Court is invoked—mainly suits between states. However, certain applications that are technically original but in fact appellate, e.g., habeas corpus motions filed directly with the Court, are included in our tabulations and analysis.

with the usual requirements of the Supreme Court's rules, which include a filing fee. The "miscellaneous docket" comprises applications for review (again, they may be either petitions for certiorari or appeals) in which the requirement of a printed submission and filing fee is waived because of the applicant's poverty. We refer to cases on the appellate docket as "paid" cases and cases on the miscellaneous docket as "indigent."[7]

All cases on the appellate docket are abstracted in *United States Law Week* (Supreme Court Section), and we used the information in these abstracts to categorize each case. The *Law Week* abstracts are very brief and often cryptic. Although our research assistants were instructed to consult the decision of the lower court or the briefs in the Supreme Court when not satisfied with the account in *Law Week,* we do not doubt that our heavy reliance on the *Law Week* abstracts produced occasional misclassifications. We experimented with going directly to the filings in the Court to determine the proper classification of each case. But apart from the tedium of the process, it turns out that extracting the issue(s) from a case, classifying the case by subject matter, and deciding whether a constitutional issue is presented involve elements of judgment; and we lacked confidence that either we or our research assistants could improve significantly upon the quality and objectivity of the work product of *Law Week*'s editors.[8]

Since indigent cases are not summarized in *Law Week,* it was necessary to go to the actual filings in the Court—many of them handwritten, and some quite incoherent[9]—to

---

7. Both the "appellate" and "miscellaneous" dockets of the Court are, of course, part of the Court's appellate, as distinct from its original, jurisdiction. See note 6 *supra.*

8. During part of the period embraced by this study, the *Harvard Law Review,* in its annual Supreme Court Note (November issue), provided a subject-matter classification of the applications for review on the appellate docket. However, because of differences in the subject-matter categories used, it has been impossible for us to compare our results with the *Review*'s.

9. However, the quality of the indigent applications has been increasing steadily due to the greater frequency of legal representation of indigent applicants. See p. 43 *infra.*

obtain the necessary data for the miscellaneous docket. To save time, we examined one out of every ten indigent applications. The figures that we present here relating to the indigent cases are ten times the actual figures derived from our sample and are thus computed rather than direct measurements.

Table 3.1 compares our data for paid cases obtained from *Law Week* and our data for indigent cases estimated by the sampling method just described with figures compiled by the Freund study group from data furnished it by the Clerk of the Supreme Court, and reveals only minor discrepancies.[10]

TABLE 3.1

Comparison of Supreme Court's Clerk's Data on Cases
Filed to Our Data—1956-1973[a]

Term	Paid Cases		Indigent Cases		Total	
	Clerk's Data[b]	Our Data	Clerk's Data[b]	Our Data	Clerk's Data[b]	Our Data
1956 ...	977	1,006	825	820	1,802	1,826
1957 ...	828	846	811	800	1,639	1,646
1958 ...	889	900	930	920	1,819	1,820
1959 ...	857	882	1,005	1,000	1,862	1,882
1960 ...	842	880	1,098	1,090	1,940	1,970
1961 ...	890	901	1,295	1,280	2,185	2,181
1962 ...	959	999	1,414	1,400	2,373	2,399
1963 ...	1,018	1,026	1,276	1,270	2,294	2,296
1964 ...	1,042	1,034	1,246	1,240	2,288	2,274
1965 ...	1,196	1,223	1,578	1,520	2,774	2,743
1966 ...	1,207	1,204	1,545	1,500	2,752	2,704
1967 ...	1,278	1,305	1,828	1,800	3,106	3,105
1968 ...	1,324	1,339	1,947	1,810	3,271	3,149
1969 ...	1,463	1,487	1,942	1,870	3,405	3,357
1970 ...	1,588	1,609	1,831	1,750	3,419	3,359
1971 ...	1,713	1,714	1,930	1,910	3,643	3,624
1972 ...	1,741	1,760	2,000	1,960	3,741	3,720
1973 ...	2,068	2,097	2,118	2,070	4,186	4,167
Total ..	21,880	22,212	26,619	26,010	48,499	48,222

[a]The data include only cases within the Court's appellate, as opposed to original, jurisdiction.

[b]Source: *1956-71:* Freund report, *supra* note 1, at A2. *1971-73:* Office of the Clerk, U.S. Supreme Court.

---

10. Here it should be mentioned that whenever a source is not given for data in our tables, the source is our own study of the cases filed with the Court in the period 1956-73, based either on the *Law Week* abstracts or on our sample of indigent cases.

2.   The Explosive Growth of the Criminal Docket

Table 3.2 presents the basic data on the composition of the caseload—and reveals a striking increase in the proportion of criminal cases.[11] In 1956, 48 percent of the docket was criminal; by 1973 the figure was 62 percent. This implies, of course, that Supreme Court criminal cases grew much more rapidly than civil. Especially rapid was the growth of criminal cases on the appellate (*i.e.*, paid cases) docket: from 181 in the 1956 term to 706 in the 1973 term, an increase of 290 percent. The entire criminal docket (including indigent cases) grew by 191 percent, and the entire civil docket by 69 percent. Given the preponderance of criminal cases in the Court's docket and its evident importance in the growth of the docket in recent years, it is plain that reforms aimed at limiting the criminal caseload of the Court could have dramatic effects on the caseload figures. It is also plain that a caseload so heavily dominated

TABLE 3.2
Civil-Criminal Composition of Supreme Court's Caseload—1956-73

Term	Civil Cases			Criminal Cases			Total Cases
	Paid	Indigent	Total	Paid	Indigent	Total	
1956 . . .	825	120	945	181	700	881	1,826
1957 . . .	688	50	738	158	750	908	1,646
1958 . . .	720	100	820	180	820	1,000	1,820
1959 . . .	695	40	735	187	960	1,147	1,882
1960 . . .	658	70	728	222	1,020	1,242	1,970
1961 . . .	686	150	836	215	1,130	1,345	2,181
1962 . . .	771	80	851	228	1,320	1,548	2,399
1963 . . .	757	140	897	269	1,130	1,399	2,296
1964 . . .	766	140	906	268	1,100	1,368	2,274
1965 . . .	844	140	984	379	1,380	1,759	2,743
1966 . . .	866	130	996	338	1,370	1,708	2,704
1967 . . .	939	190	1,129	366	1,610	1,976	3,105
1968 . . .	926	210	1,136	413	1,600	2,013	3,149
1969 . . .	1,014	190	1,204	473	1,680	2,153	3,357
1970 . . .	1,075	220	1,295	534	1,530	2,064	3,359
1971 . . .	1,120	290	1,410	594	1,620	2,214	3,624
1972 . . .	1,153	420	1,573	607	1,540	2,147	3,720
1973 . . .	1,391	210	1,601	706	1,860	2,566	4,167

11. We define "criminal cases" to include postconviction proceedings, such as habeas corpus, which are formally civil.

by one type of litigation cannot be assumed to be a simple function of population, gross national product, or other gross indicators of social activity.

It is worthwhile pausing a moment to ponder the implications of the extraordinary preponderance of criminal matters in the applications for Supreme Court review—while reminding the reader that the applications caseload is not a measure of the Court's total workload. Although we certainly do not deny the importance of protecting the procedural rights of people accused of criminal activity, we wonder at the wisdom of institutional arrangements that have made criminal review so important a part of the work of the Supreme Court, given all the other social and political issues that are within the Court's jurisdiction.

In order to analyze the growth in the criminal docket more closely, we must separate federal and state criminal matters. This is done in table 3.3. A striking result in this

TABLE 3.3
Growth in Supreme Court's Criminal Docket—1956-73

Term	Federal Cases			State Cases			Total Criminal Cases
	Paid	Indigent	Total	Paid	Indigent	Total	
1956 ...	115	150	265	66	550	616	881
1957 ...	108	230	338	50	520	570	908
1958 ...	113	220	333	67	600	667	1,000
1959 ...	117	150	267	70	810	880	1,147
1960 ...	122	300	422	100	720	820	1,242
1961 ...	122	210	332	93	920	1,013	1,345
1962 ...	123	310	433	105	1,010	1,115	1,548
1963 ...	163	300	463	106	830	936	1,399
1964 ...	157	410	567	111	690	801	1,368
1965 ...	199	390	589	180	990	1,170	1,759
1966 ...	184	370	554	154	1,000	1,154	1,708
1967 ...	193	470	663	173	1,140	1,313	1,976
1968 ...	193	530	723	220	1,070	1,290	2,013
1969 ...	246	590	836	227	1,090	1,317	2,153
1970 ...	317	610	927	217	920	1,137	2,064
1971 ...	328	680	1,008	266	940	1,206	2,214
1972 ...	377	720	1,097	230	820	1,050	2,147
1973 ...	410	770	1,180	296	1,090	1,386	2,566

table is the difference in growth rates between the federal and state criminal matters on the Court's docket. Between the 1956 and 1973 terms, the number of state criminal cases grew by 125 percent, and while this is a large increase, it is only trivially greater than the (estimated) increase in the number of state criminal convictions during this period.[12] This suggests that the dramatic increases in the rights of state criminal defendants resulting from the Warren Court's decisions in areas such as search and seizure and right to counsel may have had little or no effect on the overall demand for Supreme Court review. Moreover, as shown in table 3.4, while the Supreme Court's decisions in 1963 liberalizing the use of federal habeas corpus proceedings to review state convictions[13] evidently increased the number of applications for review arising out of federal habeas corpus proceedings brought by state prisoners, that effect appears to have been offset by a decline in the number of review applications arising out of *state* habeas corpus (and other state postconviction) proceedings.[14]

TABLE 3.4
Procedural Origin of State Criminal Cases on
Supreme Court's Miscellaneous Docket—1956-73

	Procedural Origin (%)					
Terms	Direct Review of Conviction	Federal Habeas Corpus	State Habeas Corpus	*Other Postconviction Remedies*		Total Cases in Sample
				State	Federal	
1956-58 ..	23.4	18.0	40.1	16.8	1.8	167
1959-61 ..	17.6	13.1	48.2	20.8	.4	245
1962-64 ..	24.1	17.0	42.7	15.8	.4	253
1965-67 ..	20.6	24.8	35.4	18.6	.6	311
1968-70 ..	25.4	30.6	27.4	15.6	1.0	307
1971-73 ..	37.4	41.2	10.3	8.6	2.4	243

12. We calculate a 121 percent increase in the number of "index" (*i.e.,* serious) state criminal convictions during the period (with a slight time lag, to reflect the time it takes for a criminal matter to proceed through the courts to the Supreme Court) covered by our study. 26 U.S. Federal Bureau of Investigation, Uniform Crime Reports: Semiannual Bull., 1955, at 59; U.S. Federal Bureau of Investigation, Uniform Crime Reports: 1969, at 102. The underlying statistics must be taken with a grain of salt, however, because they are limited to urban areas and may thus distort (probably by exaggerating) the rate of increase in the number of convictions for the country as a whole.
13. Fay v. Noia, 372 U.S. 391 (1963); Townsend v. Sain, 372 U.S. 293 (1963).
14. Table 3.4 is limited to miscellaneous cases because the *Law Week* abstracts on which our data for the appellate docket is based do not indicate clearly the procedural origin of the cases abstracted. Moreover, the procedural origin of the cases on the miscellaneous docket is not always clear, which is why the sample size in table 3.4 (last column) is smaller than the entire sample on which the figures in table 3.2 are based.

A major factor in the growth of the Court's criminal docket, accounting for 54 percent of the total growth in that docket between 1956 and 1973, has been the enormous increase in the number of *federal* cases on the docket. The annual number of federal criminal cases filed with the Court rose by 345 percent between 1956 and 1973 (computed from table 3.3).[15] The number of convicted federal criminal defendants grew by only 41 percent during this period[16] —much less than the growth in state criminal convictions. And while the Supreme Court enlarged the procedural rights of federal as well as state criminal defendants during this period, it did so to a lesser extent—indeed, some of the Warren Court's most celebrated criminal decisions merely extended to state criminal defendants rights already enjoyed by federal criminal defendants under the fourth, fifth, and sixth amendments.[17] Interestingly, the rate at which the number of completed federal criminal trials increased between these same years—91 percent, as indicated by table 3.5—was roughly twice the rate of increase of federal criminal defendants convicted and acquitted—44 percent—suggesting a trend to fewer defendants per trial. Whatever the explanation for this difference, the important point is the burgeoning growth in applications for Supreme Court review as compared to either federal trials or convictions. How can one explain the disproportionate growth in the federal criminal docket?

The essential clue, as revealed in table 3.5, would seem to be (1) the explosive growth in appeals to the federal

---

15. It may be objected that this computation is too sensitive to the precise beginning and end points chosen for comparison. Below we present computations based on an average of terms; they tell the same story.

	Percent Increase	
	Federal	State
1956-57 to 1972-73	278	105
1956-58 to 1971-73	251	97

16. Table H-1, Admin. Office U.S. Cts., Federal Offenders in United States District Courts: 1972. The conviction data were lagged one year, *i.e.*, comparing 1955 and 1972 (*cf.* note 18 *infra*).

17. See, *e.g.*, Mapp v. Ohio, 367 U.S. 643 (1961).

TABLE 3.5   Increase in Federal Criminal Appeals—1956-73

Fiscal Year	(1) Criminal Trials[a]	(2) Appeals Therefrom[b]	(3) (2)÷(1)	(4) Certiorari Petitions[c]	(5) (4)÷(2)	(6) Postconviction Proceedings[d]	(7) Appeals Therefrom[e]	(8) (7)÷(6)
1956	4,089	450	.110	201	.447	695	186	.268
1957	3,854	402	.104	169	.420	748	162	.217
1958	3,563	448	.126	214	.478	640	175	.273
1959	3,830	439	.115	232	.528	821	179	.218
1960	3,347	441	.132	253	.574	1,047	179	.171
1961	3,515	448	.127	250	.558	1,305	N.A.	---
1962	3,438	450	.131	245	.544	1,589	N.A.	---
1963	3,788	586	.155	270	.461	1,496	N.A.	---
1964	3,865	644	.167	341	.530	1,630	N.A.	---
1965	3,924	688	.175	322	.468	2,098	422	.201
1966	3,872	801	.207	379	.473	2,559	382	.149
1967	4,410	984	.223	415	.422	2,292	421	.184
1968	4,405	1,150	.261	458	.398	2,639	485	.184
1969	5,533	1,375	.249	535	.389	2,851	670	.235
1970	5,563	1,776	.319	642	.361	3,612	818	.226
1971	6,583	2,200	.334	568	.258	4,185	870	.208
1972	7,456	2,664	.357	904	.339	4,121	890	.216
1973	7,818	2,995	.383	1,046	.349	4,179	1,001	.240

Source: Reports of the Proceedings of the Judicial Conference of the United States, *infra* note 24, 1955-73.

[a] Trials completed in district courts during the *previous* fiscal year, *i.e.*, lagged one year (cf. note 18 *infra*). Data from table C-8 in source, 1955-60; table C-7, thereafter.

[b] Appeals disposed of after hearing or submission in courts of appeals during the fiscal year. Data from table B-1 in source.

[c] Petitions filed in the Supreme Court during the fiscal year. Includes petitions only in direct appeals from criminal trials; the number of certiorari petitions in postconviction proceedings is unavailable for appellate docket cases (see note 20 *infra*). Data from table B-2 in source.

[d] Proceedings commenced in district courts during the *previous* fiscal year, *i.e.*, lagged one year (cf. note 18 *infra*). Data from table C-2 in source.

[e] Appeals filed in courts of appeals during the fiscal year. Data from table B-5 in source, 1956-60; table B-7, 1965-73.

courts of appeals in criminal cases during the period, coupled with (2) a similar growth in federal postconviction proceedings. In 1956, only 11 percent of federal criminal judgments were appealed. By 1973 that figure had risen to 38 percent.[18] The increase in the proportion of judgments appealed from, when combined with the 91 percent increase in the number of trials, greatly dominates the modest reduction (from 45 to 35 percent) in the proportion of criminal appeals in which certiorari petitions are filed, to yield the 420 percent increase in the number of certiorari petitions filed in federal criminal cases shown in column 4 of table 3.5.[19] Nor do these figures tell the whole story: columns 6 and 7 show how the enormous increase in the number of federal postconviction proceedings has resulted in a more than fivefold increase in the number of appeals in such proceedings, a significant fraction of which result in petitions for certiorari in the Supreme Court.[20] And, unlike the Court's state criminal docket, the increase in the use of postconviction proceedings by federal prisoners has not been offset by decreasing resort to other remedies.

It is tempting to ascribe the increase in the Court's federal criminal docket to the expansive criminal jurisprudence of the Warren Court era. The increase in the use of postconviction remedies, which has undoubtedly had an

---

18. The figures in table 3.5 for the appeal rate are estimates made by dividing the number of trials (lagged one year to approximate the interval between trial and appellate disposition) (col. 1) into the number of appeals (col. 2). Data on the percentage of trial judgments actually appealed from are not available. Similarly, we lagged postconviction judgments at the trial level by one year in estimating an appeal rate from such judgments by dividing the number of appeals by the number of judgments.

19. This figure cannot be compared directly with parallel figures derived from table 3.2, because it excludes certiorari petitions to review judgments rendered in appeals from the grant or denial of postconviction relief.

20. Certiorari petitions arising from federal postconviction remedies constituted about 20 percent of the sample (55 out of 255) of the total federal criminal filings on the miscellaneous docket in the 1973 term. We do not know the comparable percentages for the appellate docket because the *Law Week* abstracts do not indicate with sufficient clarity the procedural origins of criminal cases.

impact on the Court's docket, could be traced to that jurisprudence. So, conceivably, might the increase in the rate of
federal criminal appeals: it might reflect uncertainty
engendered by the Court's innovations or perhaps even
hostility to those innovations on the part of federal district
judges. Judge Friendly ascribes the increase in the federal
criminal appeal rate to the provision of a free lawyer and
free transcript to every indigent defendant and to the
assurance that except in unusual cases the defendant who
succeeds in overturning his conviction will not be given a
heavier sentence on retrial—all conditions resulting directly
or indirectly from decisions of the Supreme Court.[21] However, these factors, if operative, should have resulted in a
comparable increase in the Court's state criminal docket,
especially given the much greater increase in the state conviction rate during the relevant period; yet, as mentioned
earlier, the state cases have increased no faster than the
number of state criminal convictions.

The decisive factor in the growth of the Supreme
Court's criminal caseload may have been the Criminal
Justice Act of 1964,[22] which provided for appellate representation, at public expense, of persons convicted of federal
crimes. The impact of the act on the growth of federal
criminal appeals (and derivatively on the number of applications for Supreme Court review of federal court of appeals
judgments in criminal cases) is suggested by the fact that,
in the eight-year period before passage of the act,
1956-1964, the number of federal criminal appeals
increased by only 43 percent, whereas in the next eight-
year period the growth was 314 percent (computed from
table 3.5). Most states provide little or no appellate representation for indigent defendants; and when they do, it is
the result of very recent reforms. This then may explain

---

21. Henry J. Friendly: Federal Jurisdiction: A General View 31-32 (New
York: Columbia University Press, 1973).
22. 18 U.S.C. sec. 3006A (1970).

the apparently much greater growth rate of federal compared to state criminal appeals.[23]

This explanation is consistent with the higher growth
rate in indigent as compared to paid federal criminal cases
on the Supreme Court's docket—413 percent versus 257
percent (computed from table 3.3). But the rapid growth in
the number of paid cases, which were presumably unaffected by the Criminal Justice Act of 1964, remains a
puzzle. The explanation for this growth may lie in a shift,
over the period covered by this study, in the composition
of federal criminal prosecutions toward types of crimes—
drug trafficking, draft evasion, etc.—that tend to involve a
more affluent class of defendants. There is evidence of such
a shift.[24] Perhaps, then, the explanation for the explosion
in federal criminal cases on the Supreme Court's docket lies
in a combination of the shift in the composition of federal
criminal prosecutions and the provisions of the Criminal
Justice Act of 1964 relating to the compensation of appellate counsel.

Thus, contrary to our own previous findings[25] (which
were limited, however, to the paid criminal cases on the
Court's docket), we are now *not* inclined to attribute the
growth of the Court's criminal docket to the Warren
Court's criminal jurisprudence as such, *i.e.*, without the
assistance of other factors. Even more clearly, that growth
cannot be attributed, save in small part, to the growth in
the crime rate. These are significant findings in their own
right, and rather surprising ones, but they do not relieve
our concern that too much of the Court's caseload may
consist of criminal cases.

---

23. We say "apparently" greater federal criminal appeal growth rate
because of the lack of statistics on the total number of state criminal appeals;
we merely infer, from the relatively moderate growth of state criminal cases on
the Supreme Court's docket, that state criminal appeals have not increased at
anything like the rate of federal criminal appeals.

24. See Annual Reports of the Director of the Administrative Office of the
United States Courts, 1956-71, at table D2.

25. See Gerhard Casper & Richard A. Posner, A Study of the Supreme
Court's Caseload, 3 J. Leg. Studies 339, 359 (1974).

Some shift in the *composition* of the Court's criminal docket due to the Warren Court criminal procedure decisions is suggested by the data in table 3.6, which lists the issue categories in which the growth of the criminal cases on the appellate docket has been concentrated. Thus, state search and seizure cases grew at a much faster rate than either the major state growth categories as a whole or the *federal* search and seizure cases—where the principle that unconstitutionally obtained evidence is inadmissible in a criminal trial had been established many years before the period covered by the table. The increase in the number of cases involving the right of confrontation of witnesses and in the number of obscenity cases are also, it would appear, legacies of the Warren Court's innovative criminal decisions.

TABLE 3.6
Major Growth Areas, Criminal Cases on Appellate
Docket—1956-73

	Average No. Cases per Year	
Issue	1956-58 Terms	1971-73 Terms
Federal cases	78[a] (112)[b]	410 (372)
Due process	9	65
Evidence	21	103
Judicial administration . .	3	23
Procedure	20	72
Right to counsel	2	20
Search and seizure	17	73
Self-incrimination	5	25
Speedy trial	1	14
Right to confront witness	0	17
State cases	31 (61)	227 (264)
Evidence	4	32
Jury	7	24
Procedure	11	53
Right to counsel	4	25
Search and seizure	4	58
Obscenity	1	34
Total	109 (173)	637 (636)

[a]There is double counting since cases raising issues in more than one subject-matter category are counted separately for each category.

[b]Numbers in parentheses represent the total numbers of cases for the period and type of case in question from table 3.3 divided by 3 to yield an annual average, *e.g.,* 112 federal criminal cases were filed on average in the 1956-1958 terms.

While it appears surprising that the state right-to-counsel cases did not grow faster than their federal counterparts or than the other major state categories, still they constituted one of the major state growth categories.

Our attempt to prepare a comparable table for the criminal cases on the miscellaneous docket hit a surprising snag: although the total number of criminal cases on that docket rose briskly over the relevant period, the number of cases in particular issue categories tended not to increase. The reason is that the number of issues raised *per case* declined over the period. The average number of criminal cases on the miscellaneous docket sampled for the 1956-1958 terms, 78, yielded 142 classifiable constitutional issues, an average of 1.8 constitutional issues per case. The corresponding figures for the 1971-1973 terms are 167 (cases), 152 (classifiable constitutional issues), and .9 (ratio of classifiable constitutional issues to cases)—a 50 percent drop in the ratio of classifiable issues to cases.[26] We conjecture that this is the consequence of the dramatic increase in the proportion of cases on the miscellaneous docket in which the applicant for review is represented by counsel. As shown in table 3.7, in the 1956-1958 terms, in only 32 out of a total of 227 cases in the sample was the applicant for review represented by counsel—14 percent; in the 1971-1973 terms this figure rose to 60 percent.[27] Evidently lawyers are more selective in tendering issues for

---

26. We emphasize that these are *constitutional* issues only. However, our results for issues classified without regard to whether they were constitutional or not are similar. Issue identification is to some extent a subjective process, but we believe that our count of constitutional issues is somewhat more accurate than our count of all issues whether or not constitutional.

27. These figures include civil as well as criminal cases on the miscellaneous docket, but only a small fraction of the cases on that docket are civil (see table 3.2). We have not made a separate breakdown for representation in criminal cases alone.

If state and federal cases are tabulated separately, the results are as follows:

Terms	% Represented by Counsel		% Not Represented by Counsel	
	Federal	State	Federal	State
1956-58	30.0	8.4	70.0	91.6
1971-73	72.2	47.3	27.8	52.7

review than laymen, perhaps feeling that meritorious issues are likely to be submerged in a sea of frivolous ones. We postpone to the next chapter our analysis of the workload implications of the dramatic increase in the frequency of legal representation of applicants on the miscellaneous docket. For present purposes, the important point is that the increase in representation makes it difficult to trace changes in the subject-matter composition of the miscellaneous docket, for many of these changes may result simply from differences in the ways in which lawyers and laymen frame issues for review. We are inclined, therefore, to place little weight on the changes that we observe in the issue composition of the miscellaneous docket.

TABLE 3.7
Representation in Indigent Cases—1956-73

| | (1) | | (2) | | (3) | | (4) | | (5) | |
| | Total | | Private Counsel | | Legal Services | | Total Represented (2)+(3) | | Pro Se[a] | |
Term	No.	%	No.	%	No.	%	No.	%	No.	%
1956 ..	70	(85)[b]	6	(9)[c]	0	(0)[c]	6	(9)[c]	64	(91)[c]
1957 ..	75	(94)	11	(15)	0	(0)	11	(15)	64	(85)
1958 ..	82	(89)	15	(18)	0	(0)	15	(18)	67	(82)
1959 ..	96	(96)	15	(16)	2	(2)	17	(18)	79	(82)
1960 ..	102	(94)	21	(21)	1	(1)	22	(22)	80	(78)
1961 ..	113	(88)	6	(5)	0	(0)	6	(5)	107	(95)
1962 ..	132	(94)	22	(17)	2	(2)	24	(18)	108	(82)
1963 ..	113	(89)	28	(25)	1	(1)	29	(26)	84	(74)
1964 ..	110	(89)	14	(13)	3	(3)	17	(15)	93	(85)
1965 ..	138	(91)	31	(22)	8	(6)	39	(27)	99	(72)
1966 ..	137	(91)	35	(26)	4	(3)	39	(28)	98	(72)
1967 ..	161	(89)	24	(15)	15	(9)	39	(24)	122	(76)
1968 ..	160	(88)	37	(23)	7	(4)	44	(28)	116	(72)
1969 ..	168	(90)	62	(37)	16	(10)	78	(46)	90	(54)
1970 ..	153	(87)	60	(39)	13	(8)	73	(48)	80	(52)
1971 ..	162	(85)	78	(48)	9	(6)	87	(54)	75	(46)
1972 ..	154	(79)	83	(54)	7	(5)	90	(58)	64	(42)
1973 ..	186	(89)	104	(56)	21	(11)	125	(67)	61	(33)

N.B. Percentages may not sum due to rounding error.

[a] *I.e.,* not represented by counsel.

[b] Percent of total indigent sample; see table 3.1 and pp. 33-34 *supra.*

[c] Percent of total in column (1).

To summarize the discussion at this point, the Court's caseload increase is due in major part to the increase in the number of criminal cases on the docket; and today, in terms of applications for review, the Court must be deemed primarily a court of criminal appeals.[28] We have also found, to our surprise, that the growth in the criminal docket is due primarily to growth in the number of *federal* criminal cases tendered to the Court for review. The number of state criminal cases has also grown substantially, but its growth has been no greater than the growth in the number of state criminal convictions; hence we hesitate to ascribe any significant part of either the federal or state criminal caseload increase to the expansion in the procedural rights of criminal defendants brought about by the Warren Court's decisions. The increase in the number of state criminal cases on the Court's docket appears merely to have kept pace with the increase in state criminal convictions (due in turn, one assumes, to the increase in the crime rate during the period), while the increase in the number of federal criminal cases on the docket appears due primarily to a combination of a shift in the composition of federal criminal prosecutions toward crimes committed by more affluent defendants and the provisions of the Criminal Justice Act of 1964 providing compensation for appellate counsel of indigent defendants.

3.   The Civil Docket

Let us turn now to the changes in the Court's civil docket. As mentioned earlier, the growth of that docket as a whole has been moderate—61 percent—in the period (1956-1973) covered by our study compared to the growth in the criminal docket. But it has certainly not been trivial. Our focus will be on the paid (*i.e.,* appellate docket) civil cases because most civil cases are paid and because the indigent civil cases have not increased any more rapidly than the paid civil cases.

Table 3.8 summarizes the term-by-term growth in the major categories of the Court's civil appellate docket. As

---

28. The composition of the merits docket is quite different, as will appear in the next chapter.

TABLE 3.8
Civil Cases Filed on Appellate Docket—1956-73

| | Cases from Lower Federal Courts | | | | | | | | | Cases from State Courts | | | |
| | Federal Government Litigation | | | | State & Local Government Litigation | Private Litigation | | | Total Federal Court Cases | | | | Total Civil Cases Filed |
Term	Review of Admin. Action	Tax-ation	Other	Total Federal Gov't Litigation		Federal Question	Diversity	Total Private Litigation		Gov't Litigation	Private Litigation	Total State Court Cases	
1956	118 (11)ᵃ	89 (4)	159 (23)	366 (14)	35 (74)	163 (5)	104 (7)	267 (6)	668 (14)	82 (83)	75 (53)	157 (69)	825 (24)
1957	92 (15)	62 (6)	100 (14)	254 (13)	34 (26)	131 (11)	105 (11)	236 (14)	524 (14)	94 (95)	70 (61)	164 (80)	688 (30)
1958	84 (12)	85 (7)	114 (21)	283 (14)	36 (64)	144 (6)	90 (14)	234 (9)	553 (15)	100 (88)	67 (45)	167 (71)	720 (28)
1959	95 (16)	70 (4)	73 (34)	238 (18)	41 (59)	165 (4)	100 (19)	265 (10)	544 (17)	89 (83)	62 (60)	151 (74)	695 (29)
1960	109 (9)	67 (4)	108 (19)	284 (12)	21 (67)	110 (4)	81 (5)	191 (4)	496 (11)	102 (97)	60 (47)	162 (78)	658 (28)
1961	107 (17)	63 (8)	90 (17)	260 (15)	32 (47)	148 (11)	88 (15)	236 (12)	528 (16)	90 (91)	68 (56)	158 (76)	686 (29)
1962	86 (13)	76 (5)	113 (17)	275 (12)	38 (53)	167 (5)	104 (13)	271 (8)	584 (13)	106 (92)	81 (56)	187 (76)	771 (28)
1963	115 (17)	50 (12)	76 (26)	241 (19)	54 (69)	149 (11)	106 (16)	255 (13)	550 (21)	132 (86)	75 (76)	207 (82)	757 (38)
1964	115 (15)	68 (9)	96 (15)	279 (13)	41 (73)	195 (7)	87 (18)	282 (10)	602 (16)	96 (86)	68 (59)	164 (75)	766 (29)
1965	126 (11)	58 (3)	106 (23)	290 (14)	50 (76)	185 (7)	109 (26)	294 (14)	634 (19)	135 (90)	75 (64)	210 (80)	844 (34)
1966	158 (8)	68 (12)	111 (23)	337 (14)	39 (64)	173 (9)	113 (9)	286 (9)	662 (15)	124 (88)	80 (70)	204 (81)	866 (30)
1967	170 (12)	55 (0)	116 (29)	341 (16)	83 (66)	192 (9)	111 (23)	303 (14)	727 (21)	132 (91)	80 (75)	212 (85)	939 (35)
1968	140 (12)	45 (11)	122 (35)	307 (21)	48 (77)	225 (9)	106 (20)	331 (13)	686 (21)	142 (82)	98 (72)	240 (78)	926 (36)
1969	143 (21)	50 (14)	131 (55)	324 (34)	124 (72)	197 (9)	103 (20)	300 (16)	748 (33)	160 (91)	106 (77)	266 (85)	1,014 (47)
1970	137 (9)	59 (14)	125 (34)	321 (20)	172 (80)	250 (11)	113 (20)	363 (14)	856 (30)	137 (93)	82 (72)	219 (85)	1,075 (41)
1971	120 (13)	55 (15)	141 (35)	316 (23)	171 (68)	229 (13)	122 (30)	351 (19)	838 (30)	185 (95)	97 (81)	282 (90)	1,120 (45)
1972	125 (24)	64 (25)	141 (35)	330 (29)	215 (69)	254 (14)	89 (25)	343 (17)	888 (34)	169 (92)	96 (81)	265 (88)	1,153 (46)
1973	198 (14)	87 (15)	150 (26)	435 (18)	193 (58)	305 (19)	137 (31)	442 (23)	1,070 (27)	218 (91)	103 (79)	321 (87)	1,391 (41)

ᵃPercent constitutional shown in parentheses.

expected, caseload growth is uneven across categories. Some have grown dramatically, some insignificantly or not at all. This impression of uneven growth will be reinforced when, later on, we examine finer categories than those used in this table.

The figures in parentheses are the percentage of constitutional cases in each category.[29] Table 3.8 reveals a significant increase in the proportion of constitutional cases on the civil side of the Court's appellate docket—from 24 percent in the 1956 term to 41 percent in the 1973 term.[30] Indeed, as shown in table 3.9, the nonconstitutional part of the Court's civil docket has grown but little since 1956; growth has been heavily concentrated in the constitutional cases.

TABLE 3.9
Relative Growth in Constitutional and Nonconstitutional
Cases Filed on the Civil Appellate Docket—1956 and 1973

	No. Cases Filed		
Type of Case	1956 Term	1973 Term	Increase (%)
Constitutional	198	570	188
Nonconstitutional	627	821	31

4.   Constitutional Cases on the Civil and Criminal Dockets

The growth in constitutional cases shown in tables 3.8 and 3.9 is all the more striking because it does not appear to be the result merely of a shift in the composition of the Court's caseload toward types of cases in which constitutional issues arise most frequently; as a comparison between the first and last rows of table 3.8 will reveal, the proportion of cases that raise constitutional issues has grown within virtually every category. These findings suggest the

29. We classify as constitutional any case in which the applicant for review tenders at least one constitutional issue, but we exclude cases in which the only such issue is preemption under the Supremacy Clause; such cases involve the interpretation of federal statutes rather than of the Constitution.

30. The growth in the proportion of constitutional cases appears to have begun well before the period embraced by our detailed statistical study. See chapter 2, table 2.7.

possibility that the increase in the Court's civil caseload may be largely of the Court's own creation since there was neither an important constitutional amendment during our period nor evidence of a trend toward greater disregard of constitutional rights by government officials. However, other factors must be considered. Changes in the political, social, or economic environment may lead to attempts to reopen apparently settled issues (such as "separate but equal") or to raise new ones (equality for women). In addition, as we shall see in the last part of this chapter, the percentage of cases that the Court accepts for review has fallen steadily over the relevant period; building on the discussion of the self-limiting character of caseload growth in the previous part, we shall argue that a possible consequence has been to reduce the proportion of marginal cases in the pool of applications. If nonconstitutional cases are, in general,[31] less important in the eyes of Supreme Court Justices than constitutional cases, one would expect the decline in the percentage of cases accepted for review to be accompanied by an increase in the ratio of constitutional to nonconstitutional cases in the applications for review. A related point is that the assumed decline in the willingness of the Court to review nonconstitutional cases may induce applicants to attempt to clothe the issues they raise in constitutional garb; these cases would show up in our statistics as constitutional cases even though they might not raise serious constitutional issues.

The impression that the Supreme Court is rapidly becoming a constitutional court is reinforced if we include the Court's criminal docket, for the proportion of criminal cases on the Court's docket that raise constitutional issues is higher than the proportion of civil cases that raise such issues, and therefore the increase over time in the ratio of

---

31. This is an important qualification. No doubt the Court considers some nonconstitutional cases (*e.g.,* antitrust) more important than some constitutional cases. Our point is only that, other things being equal, the Court may prefer taking a constitutional case to taking a nonconstitutional case.

criminal to civil cases on the Court's docket must have
compounded the growth in the proportion of cases raising
constitutional issues. Moreover, the proportion of criminal
cases that raise constitutional issues has also been rising
over time. In the 1956 term, 50 percent of the criminal
cases on the Court's appellate docket raised constitutional
issues compared to only 24 percent of the civil cases. In
1973, these figures were 81 percent and 41 percent—and
criminal cases were a larger proportion of the Court's
docket. As a result, between 1956 and 1973 the proportion
of constitutional cases on the Court's appellate docket (civil
plus criminal) almost doubled, rising from 29 percent to 55
percent (see table 3.10).

TABLE 3.10
Percentage of Constitutional Cases Filed on the
Civil and Criminal Appellate Dockets—1956-73

Term	Civil Cases	Criminal Cases			Total Civil and Criminal[a]
		State	Federal	Total[a]	
1956 ...	24	83	30	50	29
1957 ...	30	98	55	68	37
1958 ...	28	96	55	70	37
1959 ...	29	94	56	70	38
1960 ...	28	98	52	73	39
1961 ...	29	94	56	72	40
1962 ...	28	97	57	75	39
1963 ...	38	94	58	72	47
1964 ...	29	98	58	75	41
1965 ...	34	94	59	76	47
1966 ...	30	95	69	81	44
1967 ...	35	95	67	80	48
1968 ...	36	94	69	83	50
1969 ...	47	96	80	87	60
1970 ...	41	95	78	85	56
1971 ...	45	95	72	82	58
1972 ...	46	87	75	79	58
1973 ...	41	95	71	81	55

[a]Weighted average.

The predominance of constitutional cases on the
Court's docket is even greater if we include the cases on
the miscellaneous docket, most of which are criminal and
therefore predominantly constitutional. Table 3.11 shows

that today almost two-thirds of the Court's cases on the two dockets together are constitutional cases.[32]

TABLE 3.11
Percentage of Constitutional Cases Filed on Both Appellate and Miscellaneous Dockets—1956-73

	Percent Constitutional			Percent Constitutional	
Term	Method I[a]	Method II[a]	Term	Method I[a]	Method II[a]
1956 ..	54	49	1965 ..	60	65
1957 ..	62	59	1966 ..	72	66
1958 ..	63	58	1967 ..	53	67
1959 ..	70	61	1968 ..	70	68
1960 ..	69	60	1969 ..	62	74
1961 ..	63	63	1970 ..	56	69
1962 ..	72	66	1971 ..	71	68
1963 ..	63	65	1972 ..	50	66
1964 ..	66	60	1973 ..	65	66

[a]Explained in note 32 *supra.*

5.   A Closer Look at the Civil Docket

Let us now examine in somewhat finer detail the sources of change in the Court's civil appellate caseload over the period 1956-1973. Table 3.12 lists the major categories of civil appellate cases in which there was no substantial increase, or even a decrease, in the number of cases over the period.[33] In several categories the explanation for the lack of growth appears to lie in the decline or stagnation of the underlying activity. The railroad and maritime industries were declining during our period, so it is not surprising that the number of FELA, Jones Act, ICC and other Interstate Commerce Act, and Railway Labor Act

32. Two methods of computation were used in calculating the percentage of constitutional cases shown in table 3.11. Method I combines with the percentage figure for the appellate docket in table 3.10 our research assistants' count of the percentage of constitutional cases among the indigent cases that they sampled. However, they excluded cases in which the constitutional issue presented was patently frivolous. We are concerned about the subjective element involved in such a judgment. Accordingly, Method II multiplies the indigent cases in the sample by the percentage of constitutional cases on the appellate docket (see table 3.10), for the appropriate category of indigent case involved (*i.e.,* state criminal, federal criminal, or civil). The results of the two methods of computation are similar.

33. Cases from three terms were averaged together in table 3.12 in order to provide more reliable estimates for the categories involved, some of which had only a few cases in them each year.

cases also declined (or did not increase significantly), especially given the absence of other factors (such as major changes in substantive or procedural rights in these areas) that might have offset the effect on the number of cases of the decline in the underlying activity. Similarly, since the number of cases brought by the FTC and the number of antitrust cases brought by the Department of Justice did not increase significantly during our period,[34] it is not surprising that the number of cases in these areas on the Supreme Court's docket did not increase substantially either.

TABLE 3.12
Areas in Which the Civil Appellate Docket Caseload
Either Did Not Increase Substantially or Declined

| | Average No. Cases per Term | |
Area	1956-58 Terms	1971-73 Terms
Civil action from lower federal courts:		
Taxation	62	85
FPC	13	15
FTC	12	7
ICC	17	15
Immigration and Naturalization Service	8	8
Antitrust (Department of Justice)	8	11
Eminent domain	8	3
Federal tort claims	7	5
Priority of government liens	5	3
Federal government personnel	11	10
Public (federal) contracts	12	5
FELA	10	6
Interstate Commerce Act (private)	7	5
Jones Act	13	16
Patents, copyrights, trademarks	32	39
Railway Labor Act	6	6
Diversity cases	100	116
Total federal	331	355
Civil action from state courts:		
FELA	9	3
Labor relations	3	3
Total state	12	6
Total cases	343	361

34. See Richard A. Posner, A Statistical Study of Antitrust Enforcement, 13 J. Law & Econ. 365, 366, 369 (1970).

In several of the areas analyzed in table 3.12, such as federal government personnel and public (federal) contracts, the underlying activity was growing—the federal government expanded significantly during the period covered by the study—but there were no significant legal or other changes (besides the growth in the activity) operating to increase the number of cases. In these circumstances, a decline over time in the number of cases is quite possible, since the effect of the growth of the underlying activity in increasing the number of cases could be dominated by the effect of time in reducing legal uncertainty (and hence litigation) through the accumulation of precedents.[35] An important example is federal taxation. The last major revision of federal tax law prior to the Tax Reform Act of 1969 (the effects of which are too recent to significantly influence our statistics, which end in 1973) was the Internal Revenue Code of 1954. The accumulation of precedents under the 1954 Code, coupled with the activity of the Treasury Department in issuing rulings and regulations designed to clarify and particularize the application of the code, would operate to reduce uncertainty about federal tax law during the period studied. This effect might well offset the effect of the increase in the number of taxpayers and the amount of taxes (corrected for inflation) collected.[36]

The major areas of growth in the civil appellate docket are presented in table 3.13. This table explains most of the growth of that docket between 1956-1958 and 1971-1973. The aggregate growth shown in the table—331 cases—is 69 percent of the net (although not of the total)[37] increase in the average number of civil cases on the appellate docket

---

35. See figure 3 and p. 30 *supra*.

36. Also, congressional oversight is more intensive in taxation than in other areas. The tax law is likely to be amended promptly if experience reveals uncertainties that are not eliminated by administrative regulations or rulings.

37. We know from table 3.12 that in some categories the number of cases actually declined. To offset the decline and produce an overall net increase of 477 cases (computed from table 3.8), it is necessary that the growth categories have produced total gains *greater* than the net increase. Still, the categories in table 3.13 explain most of the total increase.

during this period (computed from table 3.8). The fact that nearly 70 percent of the total growth in the Court's civil appellate docket between 1956 and 1973 (based on the three-year averages) occurred in areas comprising only 14 percent of the docket at the beginning of that period demonstrates that docket growth, on the civil side, is highly concentrated in particular subject-matter areas.

TABLE 3.13
Areas in Which the Civil Appellate Docket Caseload
Increased Substantially

| | Average No. Cases per Term | |
Area	1956-58 Terms	1971-73 Terms
Military	14	30
NLRB	19	49
Civil rights acts	4	51
Racial discrimination (not elsewhere classified)	15	32
Education	1	28
Reapportionment	0	11
Elections	1	34
Health/welfare	3	32
Private antitrust	9	37
Private SEC	2	22
Government personnel (state) ...	15	44
State liquor control	2	6
Domestic relations	7	18
Zoning	4	10
Property	3	12
Torts	5	19
Total	104	435

Some of the increases shown in table 3.13 seem explicable in terms of the creation of new substantive rights—in particular the enactment of civil rights statutes and the expansive interpretation of the equal protection clause adopted by the Court during this period with respect to legislative apportionment and other matters. The increases in the number of private antitrust and private securities cases reflect the removal of various procedural obstacles to the maintenance of such actions. Consistent with our earlier theoretical analysis of caseload change, the most dramatic growth is found in areas (notably military activities, including induction, and civil rights) where rapid increases during the period in the underlying activities (due to the Vietnam War and the civil rights movement, respectively), themselves rather novel, coincided with an expansion in the relevant legal rights.

It should be noted that all important categories of Supreme Court civil appellate cases, at least as measured by the number of cases filed during the 1971-1973 terms, are listed in either table 3.12 or 3.13; any category not listed accounted for an insignificant number of cases. The Court's expansive interpretation of the first amendment has not evoked a substantial number of applications for review,[38] and the enormous legislative and judicial activity in the areas of environmental and consumer protection has not contributed significantly to the Court's caseload—or at least had not as of the 1973 term.

6.   Summary

To summarize this part of the chapter, we observed previously that there were a number of factors besides the volume of the underlying activity (crime, traffic accidents, etc.) that affected the demand for litigation in general and Supreme Court review in particular. Hence, we concluded, it could not be assumed that just because the underlying activity was growing, the number of applications for review must be growing also. The analysis in this part bears out this important point. The Court's applications caseload has grown enormously since 1956, but the growth is not evenly distributed across the various categories of cases. In particular, it has been strongly concentrated in the criminal area. Between 1956 and 1973 the Court's criminal docket grew by 191 percent, its civil docket by only 69 percent. Had the entire docket grown at the same rate as the civil docket, the number of cases filed with the Court in 1973 would have been 3,086 rather than 4,167. And, within the

---

38. With the exception of state obscenity cases, which form a growing part of the Court's criminal docket, and loyalty oath cases; most of the cases in the government personnel (state) row in table 3.13 are loyalty oath cases.

criminal docket, growth was much greater in federal than in state cases. Within the civil docket, too, growth is unevenly distributed. It is concentrated in areas, mainly of constitutional law, where the Warren Court expanded federal rights. Most of the increase in the Court's caseload seems not to be attributable to increases in population, economic activity, or other social indices (including the number of crimes committed). Rather, it appears that the increase has been, to a large extent, a product of changes in the law.

C.   Forecasting Future Caseload Changes

It should be clear by now why we reject the Freund study group's prediction "that, independent of other factors, the number of cases will continue to increase as population grows and the economy expands."[39] In the absence of "other factors" affecting the demand for Supreme Court review, the Court's caseload might remain constant or decline over time despite increases in population and in economic (and other forms of) activity.

It would appear that the most important variables in the future growth of the caseload are (1) the number and scope of new federal rights, (2) the procedural devices that facilitate or obstruct the enforcement of federal rights, (3) the costs to litigants of asserting such rights at various stages of the litigation process, and (4) the certainty or definiteness of the rights. All of these factors are at least partly within the control of the Court itself. This means that even if no measures are taken by Congress to alleviate the Court's workload, the Court might—we do not suggest that it should—take its own measures to limit its workload. It could revive notions of standing, ripeness, mootness, and the like, which limit the access of claimants either to the federal courts in general or to the Supreme Court in particular; or it could withdraw or limit some of the substantive or procedural rights that it has created by constitu-

---

39. See note 1 *supra*.

tional or statutory interpretation. Perhaps the Court's recent decisions with respect to class actions[40] and the award of attorneys' fees to equitable claimants[41] indicate that the Court has in fact begun to curtail various procedural rights in order to alleviate the burdens on it and the other federal courts. We emphasize that we do not ourselves endorse judicial convenience as a proper basis for curtailing rights.

An additional factor is the self-limiting tendency of a great volume of applications for review. As explained in the first part of this chapter, as the probability that review will be granted drops due to an increase in the number of cases filed coupled with the Supreme Court's unwillingness or inability to increase significantly the number of cases that it will review,[42] the *value* of seeking review also declines; and, other things being equal (an important qualification), the number of applications may begin to level off.

Table 3.14 shows that the likelihood of obtaining review has indeed declined significantly over the period of our study.[43] But it would be premature to conclude that

TABLE 3.14
Percentage of Applications Accepted for Review by
Supreme Court—1956-73

Term	Method I	Method II	Term	Method I	Method II
1956 ...	7.2	12.4	1965 ...	5.0	-----
1957 ...	9.3	-----	1966 ...	5.1	7.2
1958 ...	7.6	-----	1967 ...	5.2	-----
1959 ...	6.9	-----	1968 ...	3.7	-----
1960 ...	7.3	-----	1969 ...	3.7	-----
1961 ...	5.6	7.4	1970 ...	4.2	-----
1962 ...	5.9	-----	1971 ...	4.4	5.8
1963 ...	6.0	-----	1972 ...	4.4	-----
1964 ...	5.1	-----	1973 ...	4.2	-----

Source: See note 43 *infra.*

40. Eisen v. Carlisle & Jacquelin, 417 U.S. 156 (1974), discussed in Kenneth W. Dam, Class Action Notice: Who Needs It? 1974 Sup. Ct. Rev. 97.
41. Alyeska Pipeline Serv. Co. v. Wilderness Soc'y, 421 U.S. 240 (1975).
42. See table 4.5 *infra.*
43. Two methods of computing the probability of review are used in table 3.14—with discrepant results, as the reader can see. Method I divides the number of cases decided after oral argument (a proxy for the number of cases decided on the merits) by the total number of cases filed with the Court during

the declining probability of obtaining Supreme Court review has begun as yet to limit the number of applications filed. It is true, as a glance back at figure 2 will confirm, that in recent years the rate of annual increase in the caseload seems to have slowed; but there is no compelling evidence that this is the result of the falling percentage of cases accepted for review or is likely to represent more than a temporary slowdown in growth of the sort that the Court has experienced many times in the past, even in periods of generally accelerating caseload growth.

Table 3.15 summarizes the growth of the caseload in three-year periods since 1956. The sharp decline in the acceptance rate in the early 1960s shown in table 3.14 did not, so far as appears from table 3.15, cause the rate of increase in the number of cases filed to decline; whether the further sharp fall in the acceptance rate beginning in 1968 is responsible in whole or part for the decline in the rate of caseload growth since 1968 must, therefore, be regarded as conjectural.

TABLE 3.15
Growth in Applications Caseload,
3-Year Periods—1956-73

Period	Increase Over Previous 3-Year Period (%)
1956-58	21
1959-61	14
1962-64	16
1965-67	24
1968-70	17
1971-73	12

Source: Table 1.1 *supra.*

the term in question. Method II, which is based on data supplied by the Office of the Clerk of the Supreme Court to the Freund study group (and printed in the Freund report, *supra* note 1, at A2), uses the percentage of petitions for certiorari in which certiorari was granted. Neither method gives a perfect measure of the likelihood of review, and each yields a different percentage. However, what is important to our analysis is not the absolute level of that percentage but the trend; and both methods concur in showing a steady and sharp diminution in the probability of review over the period covered by our study.

Table 3.16 casts additional doubt on the hypothesis that the declining acceptance rate has begun to reduce the number of applications for review. This table is based on statistics published by the Administrative Office of the U.S. Courts showing the number of cases decided (after hearing or submission) by the federal courts of appeals, the number of petitions for certiorari in which review of a federal court of appeals decision is sought, and the percentage of those

TABLE 3.16
Petitions for Certiorari Filed and Granted from
Decisions by U.S. Courts of Appeals—1947-74

Fiscal Year	(1) Total Cases Disposed of by U.S. Courts of Appeals after Hearing or Submission	(2) Certiorari Petitions Seeking Review of Courts of Appeals Decisions	(3) Percent of Decisions in Which Petitions Were Filed (2)÷(1)	(4) Petitions Granted	(5) Percent of Petitions Granted (4)÷(2)
1947 ...	1,887	614	32.5	119	19.4
1948 ...	1,821	597	32.8	73	12.2
1949 ...	2,045	630	30.8	104	16.5
1950 ...	2,355	663	28.2	67	10.1
1951 ...	2,136	600	28.1	76	12.7
1952 ...	2,308	592	25.6	90	15.2
1953 ...	2,436	603	24.8	89	14.8
1954 ...	2,427	592	24.4	70	11.8
1955 ...	2,809	625	22.2	96	15.4
1956 ...	2,973	805	27.1	114	14.2
1957 ...	2,709	807	29.8	149	18.5
1958 ...	2,831	824	29.1	103	12.5
1959 ...	2,705	866	32.0	114	13.2
1960 ...	2,681	870	32.5	127	14.6
1961 ...	2,806	971	34.6	102	10.5
1962 ...	2,895	941	32.5	95	10.1
1963 ...	3,172	1,045	32.9	98	9.4
1964 ...	3,552	1,138	32.0	101	8.9
1965 ...	3,546	1,243	35.1	100	8.0
1966 ...	4,087	1,286	31.5	99	7.7
1967 ...	4,468	1,451	32.5	100	6.9
1968 ...	4,668	1,532	32.8	156	10.2
1969 ...	5,121	1,668	32.6	106	6.4
1970 ...	6,139	1,977	32.2	107	5.4
1971 ...	7,606	1,727	22.7	106	6.1
1972 ...	8,537	2,322	27.2	134	5.8
1973 ...	9,618	2,524	26.2	135	5.3
1974 ...	8,451	2,520	29.8	158	6.3

Source: Annual Reports, *supra* note 24, 1947-74, at tables B-1 and B-2.

certiorari petitions that the Court grants. A glance at the last column of the table will show that the percentage of petitions in which certiorari is granted has fallen dramatically since 1947. Yet the percentage of cases in which a petition for certiorari is filed has not fallen significantly— indeed, it has risen since the early 1950s.

In summary, while at some point applicants may become discouraged from seeking Supreme Court review by the long odds against getting it, there is no persuasive evidence that that point has yet been reached; and we do not know when it will be.

Any effort to predict the future growth in the Court's caseload is complicated by the recent changes in the membership of the Court that have created a distinctive "Burger Court." On the one hand, the new Court may, whether because of concern with the size of the caseload or for completely unrelated reasons, curtail a number of the substantive and procedural rights recognized by the Warren Court; this process may, as mentioned, have begun already. The long-run effect should be to reduce the number of applications for review since, as suggested in the last chapter, the Court's caseload growth appears to be due, in part anyway, to the expansive jurisprudence of the Warren Court. But the change in the Court's membership has also engendered uncertainty with respect to the probable decision of a number of issues, and the increase in uncertainty may produce an increase in the caseload, at least in the near term.

The possible retraction by the Court of substantive or procedural rights created by the Warren Court's expansive jurisprudence, the possible self-limiting effect of continued caseload growth, and the possible impact on the caseload of recent changes in the membership of the Court are but illustrations of the imponderables that must be considered, but cannot be quantified, in any responsible effort to forecast the Court's workload. Among other important imponderables, should the states grant appellate representation to indigent criminal defendants comparable to that afforded federal defendants, the predictable consequence would be a rapid increase in the number of state criminal cases on the Supreme Court's docket.[44]

To be sure, the fact that, as shown in figure 2, the Court's caseload has been growing steadily for a period of some 75 years establishes a presumption of continued growth in the future. However, the major development that in all probability underlies that trend—the steady growth in the domain of conduct regulated by federal statutory or constitutional law—may not continue. Moreover, our analysis has shown that the rate of growth in the caseload cannot be taken for granted but is the result of a variety of special factors that can change abruptly.

We conclude this chapter by reminding the reader that forecasting the future is a notoriously difficult art[45] and that forecasting the Supreme Court's caseload involves even greater uncertainty than economic and demographic forecasting. The facile assumption of the Freund study group that the large caseload increases of recent years are bound to continue if Congress does nothing to reduce the Court's caseload must be rejected. But this does not mean that there is no workload problem or that if there is one it is about to disappear. Our analysis is consistent with, although it does not compel acceptance of, the proposition that the Court's caseload is excessive and will remain so unless Congress takes measures to reduce it. Indeed, an important implication of the analysis is that should the Court's caseload level off or even decline in the coming years, this would *not* refute the existence of a serious problem—the caseload may simply become so large in relation to the Court's ability to decide cases that litigants are discouraged from seeking review by the low probability of

---

44. See pp. 41-42 *supra*.

45. The art of judicial forecasting is especially underdeveloped. For a recent and promising effort focused, however, on the trial court level, see Jerry Goldman, Richard L. Hooper, & Judy A. Mahaffey, Caseload Forecasting Models for Federal District Courts (J. Legal Studies, in press).

obtaining it. Finally, and critically, caseload as such cannot be deemed a problem of social concern. Whether the number of applications for review filed with the Court has reached or will soon reach the point at which the Court's effective functioning is threatened depends on the time that it takes the Justices to screen the applications for review and the consequences for the legal system of the denial of Supreme Court review in those cases that are screened out. These are matters considered in the next chapter.

CHAPTER 4
THE IMPACT OF CASELOAD GROWTH ON THE COURT'S EFFECTIVE FUNCTIONING

Too often in discussions of the Court's caseload it is simply assumed that the substantial increase over time in the number of applications for review received by the Court has impaired its ability to function effectively; and critics of the Court's performance, seeking an explanation for the deficiencies that they find, fasten on the growth of the caseload. We believe that the effect of caseload increase on the Court's performance is a matter for empirical study rather than for assumptions. And a statistical analysis has much to contribute to that study, although it cannot provide a conclusive answer to the question of how caseload growth affects the quality of the Court's performance.

An increase in the applications caseload could affect the Court's operations in several ways. First, it could reduce the amount of time that the Court devoted to screening each application for review. This might in turn result in more frequent errors in the screening process—that is, granting review in cases that did not merit review or denying review in cases that did. Second, the applications caseload increase could reduce the amount of time that the Court spent in the consideration and decision of those cases in which it did grant review (its "merits docket," as we shall sometimes call it), which could in turn result in a diminution in the quality of the Court's decisions. Third, the Court's limited capacity to review cases might force it to deny review in cases where in fact Supreme Court review would have been highly appropriate—for example, to resolve a conflict between two circuits or two state supreme courts. The third effect of a larger caseload should not be confused with the first. A reduction in the amount of time spent on screening each application might result in mistakes in the sense that one case might be accepted for review rather than another case that had a better claim to the Court's attention. But that is distinct from the problem created when, even though the Court might be accepting only the most suitable cases, the caseload is so large that the Court must turn away cases that should be reviewed beyond the state supreme court or federal court of appeals level.

A.   The Impact of Caseload Growth on Screening

We begin our examination of the possible effects of caseload increase on the effective functioning of the Court by attempting to translate *number* of applications for review into actual *time* spent on screening them. Because of the absence of any "time and motion" studies of the Justices and their staffs, we are forced to use indirect methods of estimation.

An immediate difficulty presents itself: unless every case tendered to the Court is identical with respect to the difficulty of deciding whether to grant review—as of course it is not—one is on treacherous ground in using caseload statistics to estimate the actual workload that the cases represent. Standardizing for difficulty is out of the question. One can, however, make one simple correction: deflate the number of indigent cases in recognition of the fact that on average they are less meritorious than the paid cases and so presumably require less screening time. Table 4.1 uses as the deflator the ratio of the percentage of indigent cases granted to the percentage of paid cases granted; multiplying the number of indigent cases by this ratio yields their "paid equivalents."[1]

---

1. The Federal Judicial Center Report of the Study Group on the Case Load of the Supreme Court (Paul A. Freund, chairman) (Admin. Office U.S. Cts. for Fed. Jud. Center, Dec. 1972) gives the following figures for the relative acceptance rates of paid and indigent cases, and we computed the ratios:

Percent Accepted

Term	Paid	Unpaid	Unpaid÷ Paid
1956	20.9	6.1	.29
1961	13.4	3.4	.25
1966	11.6	3.9	.34
1971	8.9	3.3	.37

The next step is to estimate the average time necessary to decide whether or not to accept a case for review. Table 4.1 uses two alternative assumptions—that each Justice spends an average of 15 minutes of his own time on a paid case (including discussion with the other Justices in conference) and that he spends just 9.5 minutes. The second assumption is derived from Hart's study.[2] If our estimates

TABLE 4.1
Estimated Time Required for Screening
Applications for Review—1956-74

				Hours per Week	
Term	Paid Cases	Paid Equivalents[a]	Total Cases	@15 Minutes per Case[b]	@9.5 Minutes per Case[b]
1956	977	239	1,216	5.8	3.7
1957	828	235	1,063	5.1	3.2
1958	889	270	1,159	5.6	3.5
1959	857	291	1,148	5.5	3.5
1960	842	318	1,160	5.6	3.5
1961	890	324	1,214	5.8	3.7
1962	959	354	1,313	6.3	4.0
1963	1,018	319	1,337	6.4	4.1
1964	1,042	312	1,354	6.5	4.1
1965	1,196	537	1,733	8.3	5.3
1966	1,207	525	1,732	8.3	5.3
1967	1,278	622	1,900	9.1	5.8
1968	1,324	662	1,986	9.5	6.0
1969	1,463	719	2,182	10.5	6.6
1970	1,588	677	2,265	10.9	6.9
1971	1,713	714	2,427	11.7	7.4
1972	1,741	740	2,481	11.9	7.6
1973	1,956	735	2,691	12.9	8.2
1974	1,768	700	2,468	11.9	7.5

Source: *1956-71:* Freund report, *supra* note 1, at A2. *1971-74:* Office of the Clerk, U.S. Supreme Court.

[a]Term explained in text.

[b]52-week year assumed. This assumption is discussed in the text below.

To derive the "paid equivalents" in table 4.1 we multiplied the number of indigent cases by .29 for the 1956-60 terms, by .25 for the 1961-64 terms, by .34 for the 1965-68 terms, and by .37 for the 1969-74 terms.

2. Henry M. Hart, Jr., The Supreme Court, 1958 Term: The Time Chart of the Justices, 73 Harv. L. Rev. 84 (1959). The average time we derived from Hart's estimates was actually 10.4-11.4 minutes depending on the precise mixture of cases in the term. We reduced it to 9.5 minutes after adjusting downward, from 30 minutes to 15, his estimate of the time required to dispose of a nonfrivolous appeal (as contrasted with a petition for certiorari). We made the adjustment to reflect the fact that, by all accounts, the Court does not differentiate between appeals and certiorari petitions in deciding whether to grant review.

seem very short, it must be remembered that each Justice has the assistance of law clerks[3] and that many cases are either clear grants or clear denials and hence require little time to decide.

Table 4.1 reveals significant, but seemingly tolerable, increases since 1956 in the amount of time required by each Justice to screen applications for review. The increase between 1956 and 1974 is either 4 or 6 hours a week, depending on which assumption is made concerning the time required to dispose of the average paid case. Still, these figures afford no basis for complacency. If today the screening function takes at least one working day of each week, then if the caseload continues to increase at the same rate as in recent decades, a point will eventually be reached at which the screening function occupies an intolerable fraction of the work week. A glance back at table 1.1 will show that the Court's caseload increased seven times between 1914 and 1974; should the next 60 years show a similar increase, then by the end of that period the screening function will have become patently intolerable. But, for reasons stressed in the last chapter, it cannot be assumed that the caseload will continue to increase at anything like its historical rate.

Our confidence in the calculations in table 4.1 was bolstered by discovering that our estimate that the screening function takes approximately one working day a week is identical to a figure (unknown to us when we made our estimate) arrived at by Nathan Lewin after interviewing recent law clerks.[4] Still, various objections can be made to our figures:

1. Some Justices may spend fewer than 9.5 minutes on

---

3. The number of law clerks rose from two to three during the period covered by this study, but we assumed that this increase did not enable the Justices to reduce the amount of their personal time spent on screening. That assumption is examined critically in the text below.

4. See Nathan Lewin, Helping the Court with Its Work, The New Republic, Mar. 3, 1973, at 16.

the average case. This would imply not only that the screening function was less burdensome than we have assumed but also that the social importance of retaining the function in the Supreme Court is less than is suggested by those who have objected to the Freund study group's proposal to shift part of it to another court. If Justices spend only a few minutes deciding whether to take a case, it is difficult to maintain that they are engaged in making complex and subtle strategic judgments, relating to the timing of and vehicles for major constitutional pronouncements, that are vital to maximizing the Court's effectiveness.

There is a related point. Faced with a choice between devoting more time in the aggregate to screening and less to their other duties or reducing the average screening time per case, the Justices might elect the latter course. In that event, statistics of the actual time spent by the Justices on screening, were they available, might show no increase. But it would not follow that the increase in the caseload had had no adverse effect on the Court. The reduction in the average time spent on screening a case below a 15-minute or 9.5-minute threshold might well result in an increase in the rate of error in screening, the first possible consequence, mentioned at the outset of our discussion, of caseload growth. In principle, it should be possible to determine the existence of that effect by examining the cases reviewed and those denied review by the Court. But any such analysis would require delving deeply into a variety of substantive legal questions, probably with inconclusive results; at all events, we have not attempted it.

One extremely crude proxy for error in the screening process is the number of cases in which a petition for certiorari, having been granted, is later dismissed. Sometimes certiorari is dismissed on the ground that it was "improvidently granted"; that is, the Court acknowledges having committed an error in accepting the case for review originally.[5] Sometimes certiorari is dismissed because the Justices discover a jurisdictional defect that bars Supreme Court review—but these can also be viewed as cases in which the original grant of certiorari was in error.[6] Occasionally, however, dismissal is for reasons unrelated to the soundness of the original grant of certiorari.[7] The principal objection to using dismissals as a proxy for mistakes is that, unless the mistake is discovered before the case has been briefed and argued—the atypical case, one imagines—the Court is probably more likely to decide the case on the merits than it is to dismiss the writ of certiorari as having been improvidently granted (unless the mistake is having accepted for review a case in which the Court lacks jurisdiction). Such errors will not show up in statistics on the number of dismissals. For what they are worth (little, we suspect) the statistics on dismissals show no increase over the period covered by our study, despite the substantial caseload growth during that period.[8]

Another possible proxy for accuracy in the screening process is the percentage of cases decided on the merits in which the Court reverses rather than affirms the judgment below. The theory would be that ordinarily—not invariably[9]—the Court accepts a case for review expecting to reverse the judgment below, so that if one observed a trend toward an increased percentage of affirmances it would suggest that perhaps the Court was encountering increasing

---

5. Of course, in some cases this mode of dismissal might disguise a strategic decision not to review the case. Still, this would imply that the Court had made a mistake in granting certiorari originally.

6. Unless the jurisdictional issue was sufficiently substantial to warrant full briefing and oral argument.

7. For example, the parties might have settled the case in the interim.

8. Dismissals of Certiorari, 1956-73.

Term	No.	Term	No.	Term	No.
1956	0	1962	2	1968	5
1957	4	1963	3	1969	7
1958	3	1964	6	1970	7
1959	4	1965	4	1971	2
1960	8	1966	3	1972	2
1961	4	1967	6	1973	2

9. Conflicts among circuits or state supreme courts would be an obvious exception.

difficulty in screening out the cases that should not be reviewed because they will only be affirmed. But table 4.2 reveals no such trend.[10]

TABLE 4.2

Percentage of Cases Decided by Supreme Court in Which Judgment Below Was Reversed—1956-74

Term	No. Cases Decided on Merits	No. Cases Reversed	Percent Reversed
1956	212	138	65.1
1957	268	170	63.4
1958	187	115	61.5
1959	188	117	62.2
1960	190	101	53.2
1961	190	132	69.5
1962	284	210	73.9
1963	279	213	76.3
1964	201	140	69.7
1965	240	152	63.3
1966	282	193	68.4
1967	376	278	73.9
1968	261	169	64.8
1969	240	153	63.8
1970	350	222	63.4
1971	446	325	72.9
1972	427	264	61.8
1973	355	236	66.5
1974	316	189	59.8

Source: See note 10 *supra.*

We are unable, in short, to find any quantitative evidence that the increase in the caseload has resulted in an increase in screening mistakes, either through a reduction in the amount of time allocated to screening each case or because of other factors.

2. Estimates of the time spent on screening are affected by assumptions concerning the allocation of work time among the weeks of the year. The estimates in table 4.1 are based on a 52-week work year. This may seem excessive; but since at present about 25 percent of the applications for review are screened during the summer months,[11] and

10. This table is based on our own study of reported Supreme Court decisions and includes summary dispositions on the merits as well as dispositions with full opinion.

11. William J. Brennan, Jr., The National Court of Appeals: Another Dissent, 40 U. Chi. L. Rev. 473, 479 (1973).

the summer recess (now about 13-14 weeks) is about 25 percent of the year, the weekly time estimates in table 4.1 would be unaffected by treating term time and summer recess time separately. If, however, we assume that the percentage of cases screened during the summer recess was substantially lower in earlier years, the increases in time revealed by table 4.1 would be reduced. We have no basis for such an assumption, but we shall consider its implications anyway. Suppose the Court in the 1956 term screened only 10 percent of its cases during the summer (assumed to be 13 weeks long). Then the number of hours devoted to screening per week *during the term* would be, not 5.8 or 3.7 as shown in the first row of table 4.1, but 7.0 or 4.4. This is not a large change, and in any event its significance is not obvious. The increase in the time devoted to screening during the term is smaller, true, but the difference is made up out of the Justices' vacation time and for all one knows a significant reduction in that time could reduce the Justices' productivity significantly.

3. Other things being equal, as the percentage of cases granted declines over time with the increase in the caseload, a larger fraction of the cases filed can be expected to have some merit.[12] This in turn implies a reduction in the frac-

---

12. To understand this point, consider two hypothetical cases in which the gain to the claimant if the Court accepts his case for review and reverses the judgment of the lower court is $10,000 and the cost of Supreme Court review to the claimant (in attorney's and filing fees, etc.) is $1,000. (The example does not depend on the assumption of a pecuniary stake. The assumption is made to make the example easier to follow. A more critical assumption is that the litigant is a rational calculator.) Assume that the probability of reversal, if the Court takes the case, is 60 percent and the probability that the Court will take the case, computed solely as a function of the intrinsic appropriateness of Supreme Court review and without regard to any caseload pressures on the Court, is 50 percent in the first case and 30 percent in the second. Then the expected value of seeking Supreme Court review is $2,000 to the first claimant ($10,000 X .60 X .50 − $1,000) and $800 to the second claimant ($10,000 X .60 X .30 − $1,000), and both will seek review. (This assumes that neither party has a strong aversion to risk, but the assumption is not critical to the analysis.) Now assume that, solely because of the interaction of increased case filings and limited capacity for deciding cases, the probability of the Court's accepting a case for review is half of what it would be in the absence of any time pressures. Then the expected value of seeking review in the first case drops from $2,000 to $500 ($10,000 X .60 X .50 X .50 − $1,000) but is still positive, while the expected value in the second case drops to −$100 ($10,000 X .60 X .30 X .50 − $1,000), so the second case will not be filed.

tion of cases that can be decided in a minimal amount of time. Assume that the cases filed with the Court in any term can be arrayed according to their merit and that in deciding which cases to accept for review the Court examines carefully all cases above some point on the merit scale—call it the "merit threshold." If the average merit of the cases filed with the Court increases, more cases will be found above the merit threshold, and therefore the Court will examine carefully more cases in making its selection of (a fixed number of) cases to review. To be sure, some cases have such obvious merit that the Court spends little time in deciding whether to review them, and the number of these cases will rise too. This effect produces a reduction in screening time, but we assume that it is offset by the effect of an increase in the average merit of cases filed in enlarging the pool of cases that the Court sifts carefully in deciding which ones (a more or less fixed number) to accept for review.

As we saw in the last chapter, however, there is doubt whether the basic premise of this analysis—that the declining rate of Supreme Court acceptance of cases for review has begun to limit the number of applications for review—is correct.[13] If it is not, there is no reason to believe that the average merit of the applications filed with the Court has increased and hence that the time required to screen the average application has increased. As we shall see shortly, the average merit (especially of criminal cases) may actually have fallen.

4. A related factor suggests that table 4.1 may exaggerate the increase in the time allocated to screening. The computations reflected in that table assume that the average time required to screen indigent applications for review has increased in proportion as the acceptance rate for such applications has risen relative to that for paid applications. But we saw in the last chapter that—mainly we surmise as a

---

13. See pp. 57-60 *supra.*

result of the sharp increase in the fraction of indigent applications drafted by lawyers—the number of issues tendered for review per indigent application has declined by 50 percent.[14] This reduction should have reduced the amount of time required to screen indigent applications: fewer issues per case must be researched and pondered. More generally, the increased professionalism of the indigent applications should in most cases reduce the amount of time required for a law clerk or Justice to determine whether the application presents an issue worthy of Supreme Court review.

5. Another factor also suggests that we may, if anything, be overestimating the increase in the amount of time devoted to screening: the expansion, over the period covered by our study, in the number of law clerks assigned to each Justice. In 1956 the Justices had only two clerks each; in the early 1970s, each was given a third.[15] Now it might seem that 15 minutes, and a fortiori 9.5 minutes, is the absolute minimum of time that a responsible Justice would devote to reading, pondering, and discussing the average application for review. But even if this premise is correct, it is unimportant how the additional law clerk time available to the Justices is used, so long as it is used productively! If it is used in helping the Justices with the merits docket (i.e., cases accepted for review), that frees some Justice time for screening without any reduction in the amount of total time (law clerk plus Justice time) devoted to the merits docket.

Moreover, efforts have been made recently to use clerks more effectively in screening. Five of the Justices (Burger, Blackmun, Powell, Rehnquist, and White) have "pooled" their law clerks for purposes of preparing "cert. memos," the summaries of the applications for review on which each

14. See pp. 44-45 *supra*.

15. Actually the computation of the Court's law clerk strength is more complex than we imply—the Chief Justice has additional clerks, and clerks assigned to retired Justices normally assist active Justices as well. But these refinements are inessential to our analysis and will be ignored.

Justice normally bases his decision whether to vote for or against accepting the case for review. The traditional practice was for a law clerk in each Justice's office to write a cert. memo for his Justice in each case. In contrast, one law clerk writes a cert. memo for each Justice who is in the pool—in principle enabling an 80 percent reduction in the amount of time allocated to screening by the law clerks of the Justices in the pool.

This innovation may not reduce the amount of Justice time devoted to screening—the Justice must still read the clerk's memo and, in the closer cases, the briefs on which the memo is based—but it should free considerable clerk time from the screening function for assisting the Justices in other areas of their work. We must also consider, however, the effects on clerk time of the Court's abandonment of the former practice of having the clerks in the Chief Justice's office prepare cert. memos for all of the Justices in all indigent cases. This practice was abandoned during the 1960s, consistent with the increasing professionalism of the indigent applications, which as we have seen has made them more and more like the paid applications; since then the indigent applications have been distributed to each Justice's office, resulting in increased burdens on the law clerks. Perhaps the pool has done nothing more than offset that burden and restore approximately the situation as it existed before the practice with respect to indigent applications was changed.

A final point to be noted regarding the impact of case-load growth on the screening function is that, if the growth were truly burdensome, one would expect to observe an increase in the Court's backlog, delay being a common institutional response to overwork. Table 4.3 indicates, however, that the Court's backlog of applications for review (which we define as the ratio of cases carried over to the next term to cases disposed of in the current term) remained approximately constant over the period of our study.

To summarize, it would appear that the amount of time

TABLE 4.3
Supreme Court's Backlog—1956-74

Term	(1) No. Cases Disposed of	(2) No. Carried Over	(3) Ratio of (2) to (1)
1956	1,701	351	.206
1957	1,783	225	.126
1958	1,781	281	.158
1959	1,822	356	.195
1960	1,928	385	.200
1961	2,157	428	.198
1962	2,350	474	.202
1963	2,412	367	.152
1964	2,180	482	.221
1965	2,693	591	.219
1966	2,903	453	.156
1967	2,973	613	.206
1968	3,151	767	.243
1969	3,409	793	.233
1970	3,422	790	.231
1971	3,645	888	.244
1972	3,748	892	.238
1973	4,200	879	.209
1974	3,799	821	.216

Source: Office of the Clerk, U.S. Supreme Court.

each Justice devotes to screening applications for review has increased only moderately since 1956—probably by less than 6 hours a week—and with no discernible reduction in the efficiency with which the screening function is performed. However, 6 hours is not a trivial fraction of a normal work week, and if the Justices were working to full capacity in 1956 that additional time would have to be taken from some other part of their work (presumably their work on the merits cases) unless the law clerk time that they have gained (40 or more hours per week per Justice) is equal to or greater than the 6 or so hours of Justice time lost. But this is an important "unless." Moreover, the alternative hypothesis, that the Justices were *not* working to full capacity in 1956—that they had unused capacity which they could put to work on additional screening in subsequent years without reducing the amount of time that they devote to the merits docket—cannot be rejected on the basis of any data we have been able to obtain.

B.   The Impact of Caseload Growth on the Merits Docket

We have no direct information on the amount of time that the Justices devote to the cases accepted for review, the merits docket, except for an estimate, presented in table 4.4, of the number of hours allotted for oral argument, which shows a slight increase in the last 20 years. No

TABLE 4.4
Hours Allotted to Oral Argument—1955-75

Term	Total Hours
1955	141
1960	165
1965	188
1970	176
1975	176

Source: Estimated from data furnished by
Office of the Clerk, U.S. Supreme Court.

doubt the largest amount of time allotted to the merits docket is consumed in the preparation of opinions, majority or dissenting.[16] Table 4.5 indicates, however, that the number of signed majority opinions issued by the Court per term has increased only moderately since 1956—and is no higher today than it was 30 years ago.[17] Moreover, as

---

16. This was Hart's finding in the study (*supra* note 2) mentioned in chapter 2. See table 2.8 *supra*.

17. Before 1927, when the full effect of the Judiciary Act of 1925 was first felt, the Court's annual output of signed majority opinions was substantially higher than it has been in any recent term, according to data provided to us by the Office of the Clerk of the Supreme Court.

Incidentally, the implications of table 4.5 would be unchanged if we added the Court's per curiam opinions in argued cases, for the number of such opinions is small and not growing:

Term	Per Curiams after Argument	Term	Per Curiams after Argument	Term	Per Curiams after Argument
1940 . . .	20	1952 . . .	10	1964 . . .	17
1941 . . .	14	1953 . . .	23	1965 . . .	8
1942 . . .	14	1954 . . .	16	1966 . . .	15
1943 . . .	6	1955 . . .	18	1967 . . .	17
1944 . . .	7	1956 . . .	23	1968 . . .	14
1945 . . .	4	1957 . . .	27	1969 . . .	21
1946 . . .	3	1958 . . .	23	1970 . . .	20
1947 . . .	14	1959 . . .	20	1971 . . .	24
1948 . . .	18	1960 . . .	22	1972 . . .	17
1949 . . .	14	1961 . . .	21	1973 . . .	18
1950 . . .	15	1962 . . .	19	1974 . . .	19
1951 . . .	25	1963 . . .	20		

TABLE 4.5
Signed Majority Opinions by Supreme Court—1927-74

Term	No.	Term	No.	Term	No.
1927	175	1943	130	1959	97
1928	129	1944	156	1960	110
1929	134	1945	134	1961	85
1930	166	1946	142	1962	110
1931	150	1947	110	1963	111
1932	168	1948	114	1964	91
1933	158	1949	87	1965	97
1934	156	1950	91	1966	100
1935	145	1951	83	1967	110
1936	149	1952	104	1968	99
1937	152	1953	65	1969	88
1938	139	1954	78	1970	109
1939	137	1955	82	1971	129
1940	165	1956	100	1972	140
1941	151	1957	104	1973	141
1942	147	1958	99	1974	123

Source: *1927-34, 1972-74:* Office of the Clerk, U.S. Supreme Court. *1935-71:* Freund report, *supra* note 1, at A7.

shown in table 4.6, the number of signed majority opinions per Justice is only about half the corresponding figure for the federal courts of appeals; and if per curiam opinions are added, the apparent contrast in the workloads of Supreme Court Justices and circuit judges is even more marked.

Superficially at least, it would not appear that writing on average little more than one signed majority opinion per month, with substantial law clerk assistance, should represent an undue workload, even though the Justices have other claims on their time—screening applications for review, hearing oral argument, deliberating, reading briefs, reviewing opinions drafted by other Justices, etc. But given the presumed difficulty and importance of most of the cases accepted for review, mere number of opinions may not convey the true workload pressures. Moreover, it is possible that the average Supreme Court case today is more difficult to decide than was the average case 40 years ago, as a result either of greater selectivity in accepting cases for review or of a shift in the composition of the merits docket toward more difficult cases (which could, of course, be a result of greater selectivity, but could have other causes as well).

TABLE 4.6
Average Number of Opinions per Judge: Supreme
Court and Courts of Appeals—1956-74

| Term[a] | Supreme Court | | Courts of Appeals | |
	Signed Majority Opinions per Justice	All Opinions[b] per Justice	Signed Majority Opinions per Judge	All Opinions[c] per Judge
1956	11.1	13.7	N.A.	N.A.
1957	11.6	14.6	N.A.	N.A.
1958	11.0	13.6	N.A.	N.A.
1959	10.8	13.0	N.A.	N.A.
1960	12.2	14.7	N.A.	N.A.
1961	9.4	11.8	N.A.	N.A.
1962	12.2	14.3	N.A.	N.A.
1963	12.3	14.6	N.A.	N.A.
1964	10.1	12.0	N.A.	N.A.
1965	10.8	11.7	N.A.	N.A.
1966	11.1	12.8	29.4	42.2
1967	12.2	14.1	30.5	45.1
1968	11.0	12.6	28.4	45.0
1969	9.8	12.1	32.0	49.8
1970	12.1	14.3	33.7	56.7
1971	14.3	17.0	33.1	64.0
1972	15.6	17.4	33.0	68.0
1973	15.7	17.7	31.7	68.1
1974	13.7	15.8	N.A.	N.A.

Source: *Supreme Court:* Annual Reports of the Director of the Administrative Office of the United States Courts, 1966-69; Office of the Clerk, U. S. Supreme Court. *Courts of Appeals:* William M. Landes & Richard A. Posner, Legal Procedent: A Theoretical and Empirical Analysis (J. Law & Econ., in press).

[a]Fiscal year, for courts of appeals statistics.

[b]Signed majority plus per curiams in argued cases.

[c]Signed majority plus per curiams in cases terminated after argument or submission on briefs with argument waived.

As we saw in the last chapter, the percentage of applications for review granted by the Court has fallen substantially since 1965, so assuming that the average merit of the applications did not fall during the period one might expect that the average difficulty or importance—in short, substance—of the cases accepted for review would have increased. However, the workload implications of the assumed increase in average merit or substance are somewhat unclear. They depend on the Court's criteria for selecting cases to review. If the Court wished solely to correct egregious errors of lower courts, an increase in the average merit of the applications caseload might actually enable it to find 100 or so candidates for correction more easily today than 20 years ago. Similarly, if instead the Court wished to decide solely cases of public importance regardless of their intrinsic legal difficulty, the assumed richer caseload might enable it to economize on its time by deciding only such cases today and forgoing the technically difficult cases that a generation ago may have occupied a large part of the merits docket due to a relative scarcity of cases of public importance. All this is conjecture, and our point is only that an assumed increase in the average quality, in some sense, of the applications caseload does not necessarily imply an increase in the difficulty and hence time requirements of deciding the cases accepted for review.

Moreover, the assumption that the average quality of the applications caseload has increased must be examined critically. It is possible that the average merit or quality of the applications for Supreme Court review has fallen. The reader will recall that a major area of expansion of the applications docket is federal criminal cases and that this expansion is probably due to the removal of certain barriers to appeal rather than to any increase in the number of meritorious cases.[18] In effect, the cost to a federal criminal defendant of appealing his conviction, to the Supreme Court if necessary, has fallen over the period covered by our study, and this may mean that the average merit of the federal criminal cases on the Court's docket has also fallen. Marginal cases, which might not have been pressed to the Supreme Court in a period when the obstacles to a federal criminal appeal were considerable, may be pressed when those obstacles are removed.

Even if the average merit of the applications for Supreme Court review has risen, and with it the average difficulty or substance of the cases accepted for review, it

---

18. See pp. 41-42 *supra.*

does not follow that the time required to decide the cases has increased *substantially.* No doubt a more difficult case requires more time to decide, but for us the relevant question is, how much more time? We assume that most of the time required in the decision of a case is consumed, not in considering how to decide the case, but in writing the opinion. We also assume, more controversially perhaps, that the time required to write an opinion is a function of the length of the opinion—longer opinions take more time to write.[19]

Table 4.7 shows the length of majority opinions in the Supreme Court for various terms and reveals that as late as the 1969 term the Court was using fewer words to decide the cases on the merits docket than it had used in a number of earlier periods. It is true that the 1972, 1973, and 1974 terms show a sharp increase in words compared to the 1969 term, yet even in 1974 the total number of words used to decide the cases accepted for review was fewer than it had been in 1914, before the Justices had law clerks. If dissenting and concurring opinions are included, the total number of words produced by the Court in the 1973 term was greater than in any other term in our sample; yet few students of the Court's work believe that the increasing tendency of the Justices to write separate opinions (a tendency clearly revealed in table 4.7) has increased the overall quality of the Court's work product.[20] It would seem, therefore, that the Court might make up the time it has lost to screening as a result of caseload growth by curtailing its output of dissenting and

---

19. To be sure, compression can be time consuming too!

20. We conjecture that separate opinions have become increasingly ephemeral. One way to test this conjecture might be to see whether the ratio of citations to separate opinions to citations to majority opinions has declined over time as a function of the increased propensity of the Justices to write separate opinions; if so, it would suggest that separate opinions are of declining precedential significance. However, such a study would be difficult to make because *Shepard's Citations* does not distinguish between citations to majority and to separate opinions.

TABLE 4.7
Word Output of Supreme Court, Selected Years—1894-1974

Term	Majority Opinions[a]			Dissenting Opinions			Concurring Opinions			Concurring-Dissenting Opinions			Total Output of Words (Thousands)
	No.	Average Words per Opinion	Total Words (Thousands)	No.	Average Words per Opinion	Total Words (Thousands)	No.	Average Words per Opinion	Total Words (Thousands)	No.	Average Words per Opinion	Total Words (Thousands)	
1894 ...	188	2,500	461	18	4,400	80	0	0	0	0	0	0	541
1914 ...	272	2,400	651	14	3,100	43	2	200	0.3	0	0	0	694
1934 ...	168	2,600	435	13	3,500	45	7	600	4	0	0	0	484
1954 ...	82	2,600	210	46	1,800	81	14	1,100	16	0	0	0	307
1959 ...	135	2,500	334	99	1,800	177	30	1,100	34	12	1,700	20	565
1964 ...	95	2,200	211	60	1,900	115	43	1,400	59	10	2,500	25	410
1969 ...	105	2,000	213	69	1,200	84	48	1,000	46	16	1,900	31	374
1972 ...	178	3,600	640	146	2,000	293	56	1,100	64	25	1,900	47	1,044
1973 ...	171	4,200	713	126	2,300	286	54	900	46	19	2,700	51	1,096
1974 ...	155	4,200	645	125	2,100	264	54	900	46	13	3,100	40	995

Source: U.S. Reports.

[a]Includes both per curiam and signed majority opinions.

concurring opinions. Furthermore, it is well known that law clerks play an important role in the research and writing of Supreme Court opinions. During the period covered by table 4.7, the number of law clerks assigned to each Justice grew from zero to three. It would seem that this increase in supporting personnel would have enabled the Court to increase its word output with no increase in the amount of Justice time devoted to opinion writing. Beginning with the 1976 term, a fourth law clerk has been authorized for each Justice.

It is conceivable, to be sure, that the cases that the Court accepts for review have so increased in average difficulty and importance as a result of the greater selectivity (possibly) implicit in the rising ratio of applications to acceptances that the Court should be writing even *longer* average opinions today than shown in table 4.7 for 1974. Some support for this conjecture is perhaps provided by table 4.8, which tabulates the average length of Supreme Court majority opinions in 255 leading constitutional cases,[21] grouped in 20-year periods since 1793. A comparison of tables 4.7 and

TABLE 4.8
Average Number of Words in Leading Constitutional
Supreme Court Opinions—1793-1974

Terms	Majority Opinions		Dissenting Opinions		Concurring Opinions	
	No.	Average Words	No.	Average Words	No.	Average Words
1793-1814 ..	7	6,300	0	0	9	1,700
1815-34	12	8,800	3	7,400	8	8,300
1835-54	8	5,800	9	14,000	16	3,200
1855-74	20	5,700	9	4,700	16	7,600
1875-94	17	6,600	9	5,100	3	900
1895-1914 ..	18	7,600	17	6,500	1	1,400
1915-34	33	5,300	30	3,700	1	2,800
1935-54	50	5,800	54	3,500	36	2,600
1955-74	90	6,500	101	4,500	87	2,500

Source: Kurland & Casper, *supra* note 21; U.S. Reports.

21. Collected—for completely different purposes from ours here—in Philip B. Kurland & Gerhard Casper, eds., Landmark Briefs and Arguments of the Supreme Court of the United States: Constitutional Law, vols. 1-80 (Arlington, Va.: University Publications of America, 1975-1977).

4.8 reveals that opinions in leading cases tend to be longer than the average opinion; and the fact that the average length of opinions in leading constitutional cases has been so remarkably stable over a period of almost 200 years suggests that there really is a correlation between the difficulty or importance of a case and the length of the opinion in the case.

Further light is cast on this question by tables 4.9 through 4.11. Table 4.9 shows the percentage of cases accepted for review in which one or more constitutional issues were raised. If one assumes that constitutional cases are more difficult on average than nonconstitutional cases, then table 4.9 implies that the average difficulty of the cases decided by the Court has risen over the period covered by this study.

TABLE 4.9
Percentage of Cases Accepted for Review That
Present Constitutional Issues—1956-73

Term	%	Term	%
1956	36.3	1965	42.5
1957	36.6	1966	52.8
1958	29.4	1967	54.5
1959	34.0	1968	63.2
1960	41.6	1969	50.8
1961	34.2	1970	70.3
1962	51.1	1971	68.9
1963	52.7	1972	62.0
1964	45.8	1973	54.7

Source: See note 10 *supra.*

Tables 4.10 and 4.11 trace changes in the composition of the Court's merits docket over the period covered by this study. Table 4.10 examines the gross subject-matter categories such as civil and criminal, table 4.11 some of the important finer subject-matter categories such as antitrust and first amendment rights. Except for the growth in the number of constitutional cases, it does not appear from these tables that the composition of the Court's merits docket has changed substantially over the period covered by our study. For example, despite the dramatic growth in

TABLE 4.10
Broad Subject-Matter Categories, Supreme Court Dispositions with Full Opinion—1956-74

	Civil Actions										Criminal Actions[a]			Total[b] Cases Disposed of with Full Opinion
	Cases from Lower Federal Courts						Cases from State Courts			Total Civil Cases				
	Federal Gov't Litigation[d]	State/Local Gov't Litigation	Private Litigation			Total Federal	State/Local Gov't Litigation	Private Litigation	Total[c] State		Federal Cases	State Cases	Total Criminal Cases	
Term			Federal Question	Diversity	Total Private									
1956	32 (28)	3 (3)	14 (12)	3 (3)	17 (15)	52 (46)	9 (8)	6 (5)	16 (14)	68 (60)	24 (21)	10 (9)	34 (30)	113
1957	53 (45)	1 (1)	8 (7)	2 (2)	10 (8)	64 (54)	10 (8)	8 (7)	18 (15)	82 (69)	22 (18)	14 (12)	36 (30)	119
1958	31 (28)	7 (6)	5 (4)	10 (9)	15 (13)	53 (47)	11 (10)	8 (7)	19 (17)	72 (64)	18 (16)	14 (13)	32 (29)	112
1959	48 (46)	1 (1)	17 (16)	2 (2)	19 (18)	68 (65)	7 (7)	3 (3)	10 (10)	78 (74)	16 (15)	7 (7)	23 (22)	105
1960	40 (34)	10 (8)	10 (8)	3 (3)	13 (11)	63 (53)	15 (13)	5 (5)	20 (17)	83 (70)	23 (19)	11 (9)	34 (29)	118
1961	26 (27)	5 (5)	18 (19)	4 (4)	22 (23)	63 (55)	10 (10)	5 (5)	17 (18)	70 (73)	11 (11)	14 (15)	25 (26)	96
1962	36 (31)	7 (6)	17 (15)	2 (2)	19 (16)	62 (53)	11 (9)	11 (9)	23 (20)	85 (73)	12 (10)	19 (16)	31 (26)	117
1963	37 (29)	15 (12)	15 (12)	6 (5)	21 (17)	73 (57)	7 (6)	11 (9)	19 (15)	92 (72)	17 (13)	17 (13)	34 (27)	127
1964	41 (36)	5 (4)	16 (14)	6 (5)	22 (19)	68 (60)	3 (3)	6 (5)	9 (8)	77 (68)	10 (9)	24 (21)	34 (30)	114
1965	33 (31)	6 (6)	15 (14)	5 (3)	20 (19)	59 (55)	6 (6)	2 (2)	9 (8)	68 (64)	16 (15)	22 (21)	38 (36)	107
1966	43 (36)	11 (9)	14 (12)	4 (3)	18 (15)	72 (61)	4 (3)	3 (3)	8 (7)	80 (67)	7 (6)	32 (27)	39 (33)	119
1967	34 (27)	7 (6)	19 (15)	3 (2)	22 (17)	63 (50)	13 (10)	6 (5)	19 (15)	82 (65)	16 (13)	27 (21)	43 (34)	127
1968	27 (23)	16 (13)	12 (10)	4 (3)	16 (13)	59 (49)	6 (5)	5 (4)	11 (9)	70 (58)	19 (16)	29 (24)	48 (40)	120
1969	22 (23)	19 (20)	14 (15)	0 (0)	14 (15)	55 (59)	2 (2)	3 (3)	5 (5)	60 (64)	13 (14)	18 (19)	31 (33)	94
1970	31 (25)	25 (20)	11 (9)	2 (2)	13 (11)	69 (57)	9 (7)	5 (4)	16 (13)	85 (70)	16 (13)	17 (14)	33 (27)	122
1971	33 (22)	28 (19)	19 (13)	2 (1)	21 (14)	82 (54)	4 (3)	2 (2)	7 (5)	89 (59)	13 (9)	40 (26)	53 (35)	151
1972	51 (31)	35 (21)	11 (7)	1 (1)	12 (7)	98 (60)	15 (10)	1 (1)	16 (10)	114 (70)	20 (12)	27 (16)	47 (29)	164
1973	37 (24)	32 (20)	21 (13)	3 (2)	24 (15)	93 (59)	15 (10)	6 (4)	21 (13)	114 (73)	21 (13)	20 (13)	41 (26)	157
1974	42 (31)	25 (18)	18 (13)	1 (1)	19 (14)	86 (63)	6 (4)	7 (5)	13 (9)	99 (72)	19 (14)	17 (12)	36 (26)	137

Source: Supreme Court Notes, Harv. L. Rev., vols. 71-89, Nov. issues.

[a] Including collateral attack.

[b] The totals in the final column exceed the sum of the Civil and Criminal categories in all but one year, due to the omission of such categories as admiralty, bankruptcy, original jurisdiction, and federal habeas corpus for military prisoners, which contain an insignificant number of cases in most years.

[c] The totals in this column may exceed the sum of the two subcategories, due to the omission of federal government litigation, which accounts for an insignificant number of cases.

[d] The percentage of the total in the final column is shown in parentheses.

TABLE 4.11 Selected Fine Subject-Matter Categories, Supreme Court Dispositions with Full Opinion—1956-74

Term	Original Juris-diction	Federal Taxation	Review of Federal Admin. Action	Anti-trust	Civil Rights	Equal Protection	First Amend-ment	Due Process	Labor Relations	Patents	Search and Seizure	Self-Incrim-ination	Total Accounted for by Included Categories	Total[a] Dispo-sitions with Full Opinion
1956	0	6 (5)[b]	13 (12)	3 (3)	0	0	0	0	0	0	0	0	22 (19)	113
1957	0	10 (8)	24 (20)	3 (3)	0	0	1 (1)	0	3 (3)	0	0	0	41 (34)	119
1958	0	5 (4)	13 (12)	6 (5)	0	0	0	0	2 (2)	0	3 (3)	0	29 (26)	112
1959	1 (1)	12 (11)	18 (17)	2 (2)	0	0	3 (3)	0	0	0	4 (4)	0	40 (38)	105
1960	1 (1)	8 (7)	16 (14)	5 (4)	0	0	2 (2)	0	0	0	2 (2)	2 (2)	36 (31)	118
1961	0	5 (5)	12 (13)	5 (5)	0	0	0	0	7 (7)	0	0	0	29 (30)	96
1962	1 (1)	6 (5)	16 (14)	7 (6)	1 (1)	0	1 (1)	3 (3)	8 (7)	0	0	0	43 (37)	117
1963	0	5 (4)	17 (13)	8 (6)	2 (2)	1 (1)	3 (2)	7 (6)	7 (6)	0	3 (2)	0	53 (42)	127
1964	2 (2)	10 (9)	17 (15)	4 (4)	0	1 (1)	4 (4)	6 (5)	8 (7)	1 (1)	2 (2)	0	55 (48)	114
1965	1 (1)	5 (5)	12 (11)	8 (7)	2 (2)	1 (1)	3 (3)	2 (2)	4 (4)	1 (1)	1 (1)	1 (1)	41 (38)	107
1966	0	3 (3)	30 (25)	5 (4)	1 (1)	1 (1)	1 (1)	8 (7)	1 (1)	2 (2)	11 (9)	0	63 (53)	119
1967	1 (1)	2 (2)	16 (13)	9 (7)	5 (4)	0	4 (3)	0	0	1 (1)	7 (6)	5 (4)	50 (39)	127
1968	0	4 (3)	12 (10)	8 (7)	1 (1)	6 (5)	7 (6)	2 (2)	0	0	8 (7)	5 (4)	53 (44)	120
1969	2 (2)	4 (4)	10 (11)	3 (3)	5 (5)	1 (1)	3 (3)	0	5 (5)	1 (1)	2 (2)	3 (3)	39 (41)	94
1970	2 (2)	3 (2)	12 (10)	4 (3)	7 (6)	4 (3)	11 (9)	8 (7)	3 (2)	1 (1)	5 (4)	2 (2)	62 (51)	122
1971	2 (1)	4 (3)	16 (11)	5 (3)	4 (3)	6 (4)	10 (7)	12 (8)	1 (1)	1 (1)	3 (2)	1 (1)	67 (44)	151
1972	2 (1)	7 (4)	13 (8)	5 (3)	7 (4)	8 (5)	9 (5)	8 (5)	1 (1)	0	3 (2)	1 (1)	64 (39)	164
1973	2 (1)	6 (4)	10 (6)	9 (7)	9 (6)	14 (9)	12 (8)	6 (4)	6 (4)	1 (1)	5 (3)	2 (1)	78 (50)	157
1974	1 (1)	2 (1)	14 (10)	9 (7)	4 (3)	2 (1)	5 (4)	9 (7)	1 (1)	0	3 (2)	0	50 (36)	137

Source: See table 4.10.

[a]From table 4.10.

[b]The percentage of the total in the final column is shown in parentheses. Percentages may not sum due to rounding error.

the number of criminal applications for review, the fraction of criminal cases on the merits docket has not increased—in fact it has decreased in recent years.

Moreover, tables 4.7 and 4.8 imply that the pressures of time have not caused the Court to reduce the length of its opinions below some optimal level. Such an effect would have shown up in that table as a reduction over time in the average length of opinions, but no such trend is discernible. It thus does not appear that the Court is slighting its opinion-writing responsibilities as a result of time pressures.

C. The Impact of Caseload Growth on Conflicts Cases

The focus thus far has been on the time effects of the caseload increase, and we have been unable to find compelling statistical evidence that the caseload increase has eaten deeply into the time available to the Justices to discharge their various responsibilities. Now we ask whether the principal adverse effect of the caseload increase may not have been to prevent the Court from accepting for review cases that ought to receive judicial attention beyond the level of the state supreme court or federal court of appeals.

The Court has economized on its time mainly, it would appear, by refusing to increase, in proportion to the caseload increase, the number of cases to which it accords the full, time-consuming treatment of an argued case. This may be thought to imply, as we saw earlier, that the average merit of the cases accepted for review is rising, in which event some cases that would have been accepted for review 20 years ago are being refused review today. Moreover, even if, as we earlier speculated might be the case, the average merit of the applications for review is *not* rising, still, because the total number of applications has risen, presumably the absolute number (though not the proportion) of meritorious cases denied review is greater today than it was 20 years ago. Even so, however, it would not follow that there was a *problem* today, for the Court in 1956 may have been accepting more cases than it needed to accept.

Statistics can cast some light on this question. The Court's inability to review cases that warrant Supreme Court review should show up in a count of the number of cases involving a conflict among the circuits (or among state supreme courts—on a federal question of course) in which review was denied. One may doubt whether there is, in general, an acute need for further appellate review of cases in which the circuits (or, where appropriate, state supreme courts) are in agreement. All of the circuits might, of course, be wrong on a question, but it is unlikely that there are many questions on which Supreme Court review is necessary that would not provoke some disagreement among circuits. There are exceptions, of course,[22] but it is with central tendencies that we are concerned here.

To be sure, this conclusion is based on a view of the Court's function that emphasizes its role in clarifying and harmonizing federal law, rather than in correcting erroneous decisions. Like most students of the Court, we believe that the Supreme Court does not sit merely to give litigants a second (or in some cases third or even fourth) opportunity for appellate review of their case. If, however, that is viewed as an appropriate function of the Court, then clearly any decrease in the percentage of cases accepted for review is cause for concern because such a decrease is likely to impair the performance of that function.

Assuming that the absence of a conflict among lower courts is prima facie a good reason for denying Supreme Court review, the converse does not follow: the existence of a conflict among circuits or state supreme courts does not necessarily demonstrate a failure of the Supreme Court to perform its duty. If the conflict is of relatively recent origin, the Court will often be well advised to stay its hand and allow a period of experimentation with the conflicting rules, for a period of experimentation may yield valuable

---

22. *E.g.*, when the question is for some reason geographically specified so that it can arise in only one state or circuit.

information for an ultimate resolution of the conflict.[23]
Yet a rising incidence of unresolved conflicts would be
some evidence, at least, that the Court, perhaps as a result
of its growing caseload, was encountering increasing difficulty in accepting for review every case in which appellate
review beyond the state supreme court and federal court of
appeals levels was desirable.

Our research assistants took a one-in-ten sample of the
applications for review on the Court's appellate docket in
three early (1958-1960) and the last three (1971-1973)
terms covered by our study. They examined the petition
for certiorari or jurisdictional statement in each case, and
any responses thereto, for three things: (1) a conflict,
either among circuits or with/among state supreme courts,
alleged by the applicant for review; (2) a conflict the
research assistant *found*—that is, he considered the allega-
tion substantial; and (3) a conflict *acknowledged* to be such
by at least one of the courts whose decision was relied
upon by the applicant for review as demonstrating a
conflict.

The results are presented in table 4.12, which reveals
several interesting points about the conflict cases. First, in
absolute numbers, the growth of cases in which a conflict is
alleged has been only moderate over the period covered by
the study—from an average of 273 cases per term during
the 1958-1960 period to an average of 407 cases in the
1971-1973 terms.[24] Although the applications docket as a
whole has, of course, grown at a rapid rate, the percentage
of cases in which a conflict is alleged has actually declined
from 30.8 percent to 22.7 percent. Second, the number of
apparently meritorious conflict cases—cases in which either
our research assistants found a genuine (as distinct from

23. A traditional justification for federalism is the opportunity it affords
for experimentation. But federal law applies nationwide and is of growing
importance relative to state law. Thus there is a place for "regional federalism"
based on the circuits.

24. These are estimates obtained by multiplying the number of cases in the
sample (table 4.12) by 10 and then dividing by 3 since table 4.12 presents
three-term totals of a one-in-ten sample.

TABLE 4.12
Proportion of Cases on Supreme Court's Docket Involving Conflicts Among
Circuits or State Supreme Courts—1958-60 and 1971-73

	1958-60				1971-73			
	No. Cases	% of Total Appli- cations	% of Alleged Conflicts	% of Definite (Found) Conflicts		No. Cases	% of Total Appli- cations	% of Alleged Conflicts	% of Definite (Found) Conflicts
Total applications for review (sample size)	266	—	—	—		537	—	—	—
Applications alleging a conflict	82	30.8	—	—		122	22.7	—	—
Applications found to present a conflict	23	8.6	28.0	—		21	3.9	17.2	—
Applications in which lower court acknowl- edged conflict	14	5.3	17.1	60.9		15	2.8	12.3	71.4
Applications found to present a conflict that were accepted for review	17	6.4	20.7	73.9		14	2.6	11.5	66.7

Source: See text at p. 87.

merely alleged) conflict or one of the lower courts acknowledged a conflict—has remained constant; the average number of found conflicts per term actually fell, from 77 to 70, while the number of acknowledged conflicts rose only from 47 to 50. This constancy has in turn enabled the Court to handle roughly as many conflict cases today as in the earlier period. As shown in the bottom row of table 4.12, in the 1958-1960 terms the Court accepted for review 74 percent of the cases in which our research assistants found an actual conflict; in the 1971-1973 terms this percentage declined, but only slightly, to 67 percent.

Our research assistants found that 3.9 percent of the applications for review filed with the Court during the 1971-1973 terms involved a genuine conflict, but most of these were accepted for review; cases in which a conflict was found but the Court declined to review amounted to only 1.3 percent of the total cases in the sample. This result is somewhat at variance with a study of the conflict problem that Feeney conducted for the Commission on Revision of the Federal Court Appellate System ("Hruska commission").[25] His study found that about 4.5 percent[26] of the cases on the appellate docket in which review is denied involved serious—what he calls direct—conflicts among circuits or state supreme courts. However, after subtracting various doubtful cases (e.g., where there was a procedural obstacle to Supreme Court review), Feeney ended by projecting only 48 "unduplicated, unresolved and without serious procedural problems" conflicts in the 1972 term,[27] which is 2.6 percent of the total applications for review filed that term.

The discrepancy between Feeney's results and ours arises, we conjecture, from our effort to minimize the

---

25. Floyd Feeney, Conflicts Involving Federal Law: A Review of Cases Presented to the Supreme Court, in Commission on Revision of the Federal Court Appellate System, Structure and Internal Procedures: Recommendations for Change 93 (Washington, D.C., June 1975) [hereinafter cited as Hruska commission].

26. This is our estimate. The Feeney study, id., does not present percentages and they are sometimes difficult to extract from his data.

27. Id. at 108.

element of subjective judgment involved in determining the existence of a conflict. To this end we instructed our research assistants to "find" a conflict only where there was no room for doubt that a genuine conflict existed. That is why acknowledged conflicts (in table 4.12) are such a high percentage of the conflicts found. We followed and defend this procedure because, while it underestimates the number of genuine conflict cases, it yields a more accurate picture of the *trend* in the number of cases. Since Feeney was not interested in trends (his study is limited to a recent sample of cases and contains no information on earlier years), he was willing to attempt a more qualitative assessment of alleged conflicts.

The true number of genuine conflicts that the Court does not resolve probably lies somewhere between our 1.3 percent and Feeney's 2.6 percent. But even if Feeney's figure is accepted as a precise estimate, it tells us nothing about the impact of caseload growth, for he has no information on the situation 20 years ago. It cannot be assumed that the percentage of applications for review that involve a genuine conflict has remained constant—let alone that the percentage has risen—over the period covered by our study, for if the figures in table 4.12 tell us anything, they tell us that it has declined.

Feeney regarded his findings on the number of unresolved conflicts as compelling evidence that the Court is failing to discharge its responsibilities, a conclusion in which the Hruska commission fully concurs.[28] Yet his own statistics cast doubt on the correctness of his conclusion. Table 4.13 shows the length of time that elapsed between the denial of review by the Supreme Court and the resolu-

---

28. See Hruska commission, *supra* note 25, at 16-19. Another statistical study on which the commission relied was a study of dissents from the denial of certiorari. See *id.* at 19-21, 133-43. We regard the growth in these dissents as the weakest possible evidence of inability to review all cases that merit review, since it is only in recent years that Justices have made public such dissents and the practice in this regard continues to vary, in a fashion largely unknown, among the Justices.

tion of the conflict either by the Court in a later decision or in some other way (the numbers are Professor Feeney's; the percentages were computed by us). Only about a quarter of the cases were unresolved after three years. Yet surely a period of experimentation longer than three years will often represent a justifiable postponement of the definitive resolution of an issue.

TABLE 4.13
Duration of Conflicts After Denial of Supreme Court Review—1971-72

	None	1 Day to 1 Year	1-2 Years	2-3 Years	More than 3 Years	Total
No. cases	13	7	12	35	23	90
Percent of total	14.4	7.8	13.3	38.9	25.6	100

Source: Hruska commission, *supra* note 25, at 105.

Surprisingly, the Hruska commission disregarded the largely negative findings of its "consumer survey"—a questionnaire designed to elicit the opinions of leading practicing attorneys with regard to any problems of unsettled issues, conflicts, or undue delays in the areas of practice in which they specialize.[29] In general, the respondents did not think that unresolved conflicts among the circuits or state supreme courts posed a serious problem in their practice. The principal exception is one that proves the rule: patents. The fact that the validity of a patent is determined anew in every infringement suit means that sometimes a patent is held valid in one circuit and invalid in another. This is a problem, but no one thinks the solution is for the Supreme Court to pass on the validity of individual patents!

Former Solicitor General Erwin N. Griswold has stated that in recent years there were about 20 federal government cases every year that he thought were worthy of Supreme Court review but which he did not ask the Court to review because he knew that the pressures on the Court were such that it probably would not be able to take the

29. See *id.* at 144-68.

cases.[30] However, in the absence of information about the nature of these 20 cases, it is extremely difficult to determine whether 20 is a large number or a modest one.

To summarize this chapter, there is statistical evidence that the increase in the caseload over the last 20 years has resulted in a significant, though perhaps moderate (especially when the increase in the number of law clerks is taken into account), increase in the time required by the Justices to screen the applications for review. There is no compelling quantitative (or, we might add, qualitative) evidence either that this increase in time pressure has interfered significantly with the ability of the Court to discharge its various responsibilities or that the Court is denying review in cases where Supreme Court review would serve an important function.

---

30. Erwin N. Griswold, Rationing Justice—the Supreme Court's Caseload and What the Court Does Not Do, 60 Cornell L. Rev. 335, 344 (1975).

CHAPTER 5
REMEDIES FOR THE WORKLOAD PROBLEM

The statistical analysis in chapter 4 suggests that the effect of the growth of the Supreme Court's caseload on the Court's ability to discharge its responsibilities effectively has not reached—not yet, anyway—such crisis proportions as would justify far-reaching changes in the jurisdiction or structure of the Court or of the federal appellate system generally. Moreover, we saw in chapter 3 that it cannot be assumed merely because the Court's caseload has increased steeply over the past 20 years or so that it will continue to do so at the same rate. The present chapter argues that even if the workload problem is deemed already to have reached substantial proportions, the adoption of any of the far-reaching proposals that have been made for solving it would be unwarranted. Some of the proposals would not contribute substantially to the solution of the problem and others would create other problems that might be as serious as the one solved. Moreover, the proponents of radical change in this area have overlooked the possibility of more modest reforms that could solve the problem—or at least buy time to permit a more careful exploration of permanent solutions.

In the first part of this chapter we consider in some detail the major proposals that have been made by previous students of the workload problem. In the second part we consider additional proposals, our own and others', that, while not as yet a part of the agenda of discussion, seem as or more worthwhile than those that are. Among our own suggestions for dealing with the problem the most important is that the Court adopt clear guidelines for the grant and denial of review that will both enable it to reduce the number of unimportant cases that it decides (a number we believe to be very great today) and enable counsel to recognize when seeking review would be very costly in relation to the potential gains because denial is almost certain.

Our criterion for evaluating a proposed reform is a simple one: will it enable the Justices to increase their productivity by freeing a substantial amount of their time?

A.   Existing Proposals

1. The Freund Study Group's Proposal. □□ Although at the moment public attention is riveted on the proposals of the Hruska commission,[1] several earlier proposals deserve detailed attention as policy alternatives. We begin the discussion with the proposals of the Freund study group, which inaugurated the modern round of controversy over the Supreme Court's workload.

The Freund study group, while also recommending certain jurisdictional reforms, focused mainly on a new screening mechanism:

> We recommend creation of a National Court of Appeals which would screen all petitions for review now filed in the Supreme Court, and hear and decide on the merits many cases of conflicts between circuits. Petitions for review would be filed initially in the National Court of Appeals. The great majority, it is to be expected, would be finally denied by that court. Several hundred would be certified annually to the Supreme Court for further screening and choice of cases to be heard and adjudicated there. Petitions found to establish a true conflict between circuits would be granted by the National Court of Appeals and the cases heard and finally disposed of there, except as to those petitions deemed important enough for certification to the Supreme Court.[2]

We put to one side the crucial question whether the increase in the Supreme Court's caseload in recent years has, as assumed but not established by the Freund group, weakened the Court. Even if the answer is "yes" (our answer, it should be clear to the reader by now, is "not proven"), the Freund group's proposed solution is unsuited to the character of the problem. In chapter 4 we found

---

1. Discussed at pp. 102-108 *infra.*
2. Federal Judicial Center Report of the Study Group on the Case Load of the Supreme Court (Paul A. Freund, chairman), at 18 (Admin. Office U.S. Cts. for Fed. Jud. Center, Dec. 1972) [hereinafter cited as Freund report].

that the rise in the caseload has increased—but not by a great amount—the time that the Justices do or should spend on screening. The proposed national court of appeals might enable only a modest saving in that time because the Supreme Court would still be required to screen the non-obvious cases, and these might consume most of the time allocated to the screening function today.

The Freund group estimated (on what basis is not revealed) that 400 cases would survive the initial screening by the national court of appeals.[3] Assuming that each Justice would spend an average of half an hour in the study and discussion of each such case,[4] the total hours devoted to screening would be 4 a week, resulting in a time saving of only 3.5 hours a week if one accepts the lesser of our two estimates of the time currently allocated by the Justices to screening cases.[5] This, however, is presumably a minimum estimate of the potential time saving:

First, the final screening by the Supreme Court of the cases referred to it by the national court of appeals might not require much more time per case than the Court devotes to screening today, since all of the "obvious" acceptances would be included among the referred cases and since the national court's prescreening of the nonobvi-ous cases that it referred to the Supreme Court might facili-tate the Court's own screening by furnishing a concise statement of the reasons pro and con acceptance. These statements would carry a certain weight since the national court would presumably become expert in the screening function. Thus our assumption of one half hour of Supreme Court screening per case may be too high.

---

3. *Id.* at 21.

4. Some would of course be clear grants, but most would be plausible candidates for review that the Supreme Court would have to examine carefully in order to pick the 100 or so that it would review. This assumes that the Freund group's proposal would not result in the Supreme Court's accepting a substantially larger number of cases for review than it does at present. This assumption is examined in the text below.

5. See table 4.1 *supra.*

Second, the Supreme Court might not have to screen as many as 400 cases, depending on the national court's ability to anticipate correctly the Supreme Court's preferences with regard to which cases to accept for review.

Third, the caseload will presumably continue to grow, for at least a limited period of time, even if the *rate* of growth declines.

Thus adoption of the Freund study group's proposal might lead to either an immediate or eventual time saving of more than 3.5 hours per week. This is, of course, conjectural.

Another consequence of the caseload increase, as pointed out in the last chapter, is a possible reduction in the number of meritorious cases accepted for review. However, the only proposal of the Freund study group specifically addressed to this problem is one to empower the national court of appeals to resolve conflicts among the federal courts of appeals. But there are no more than 25-50 cases a year involving a conflict among the circuits or state supreme courts, and many of these conflicts are not ready for final resolution but should be allowed to simmer awhile.[6]

Other proposals of the study group, however, bear indirectly on the problem of meritorious cases denied review because of the size of the caseload. For example, the elimination of direct appeals from district courts would enable plenary review by the federal courts of appeals of many decisions that the Supreme Court today disposes of summarily (which we consider to be the equivalent, in general, of no review). Moreover, there is the question (left unanswered by the study group) what the Supreme Court would do with the time saving effected by the creation of the national court of appeals. If the time saved were used to hear and decide cases denied review today because of limitations of time, the problem (if there is one) of non-review of worthy cases would be lessened.

---

6. See pp. 86-87, 90-91 *supra*.

Conceivably, the time the Supreme Court spends on screening each case would also be reduced—it would not have to be quite so selective since it was accepting more cases. But we doubt that the time saving in screening would be large enough to produce significant effects along these lines. And it is of course possible—and we think envisaged by the members of the Freund study group—that the Court would devote all or most of any time saved to additional deliberation in cases accepted for review rather than to deciding additional cases.

The jurisdictional changes recommended by the Freund study group include, as just mentioned, the elimination of direct appeals from three-judge district courts (which would be abolished) and from one-judge district courts in government antitrust cases. Data gathered by the Freund study group show that appeals from three-judge district courts were less than 3 percent of all the cases filed with the Court during the 1971 term, but were 22 percent of the cases argued orally before the Court[7]—which suggests that this jurisdictional change could have as much impact on the Court's workload as the proposed national court of appeals. A simple calculation yields a better idea of the potential effect. Using the 22 percent figure and treating the number of cases decided with full opinion during the 1971 term (151) as approximately equivalent to the number of cases argued orally, we calculate that 33 of the cases argued orally that term were appeals from three-judge courts. The stability of this proportion from year to year, noted in the report of the Freund study group, was further verified by our data for the 1974 term, during which 32 direct appeals constituted 23 percent of the 132 cases decided by the Court with full opinion after oral argument.

To be sure, it is possible that, even if direct appeals were abolished, many of the appeals now taken directly to the Supreme Court would come there on certiorari after

7. Freund report, *supra* note 2, at 29.

review in the court of appeals. Suggestive in this regard is the fact that the total number of direct appeals filed during the 1971 term was 120,[8] which means that roughly three-fourths of all appeals from three-judge courts were disposed of summarily. This in turn suggests that the Court is already fairly selective, which implies that many cases now decided by three-judge district courts would be accepted for review if brought to the Court by writ of certiorari after court-of-appeals review following judgment by a single-judge district court. Suppose that half of the 33 direct appeals in the 1971 term would have survived in this manner. Then the proposed jurisdictional change (if effective) would have eliminated 17 cases, or 11 percent of those argued orally—a figure by no means negligible, but small.[9]

Since this proposal is relatively uncontroversial we do not discuss it further here.[10] For the same reason we do not discuss the proposal to move the remaining appeals to the discretionary jurisdiction of the Supreme Court. The Freund group rightly assumed that this reform would be more in the nature of a ratification of existing practice than a change.

2. *The Haynsworth Proposal.* □□ A more radical jurisdictional proposal is that of Judge Haynsworth, who favors "the creation by the Congress of a national court of [criminal] appeals having jurisdiction to review on writs of

---

8. *Id.* at A11.

9. The figure is larger if government antitrust cases which come to the Supreme Court on direct appeal from a single-judge district court, such as federal antitrust equity actions, are added; in the 1971 term, 32 percent of all of the cases argued orally in the Supreme Court were direct appeals from federal district courts. This would suggest that the proposed jurisdictional change might eliminate about 16 percent of the argued cases. Congress has since moved to restrict direct appeals in antitrust cases. See Antitrust Procedures and Penalties Act sec. 5, 15 U.S.C. sec. 29 (Supp. IV, 1974).

10. Congress has enacted a major restriction on the availability of three-judge district courts. The Act of Aug. 12, 1976, Pub. L. No. 94-381, 90 Stat. 1119, has generally eliminated the requirement of a three-judge court in cases seeking to enjoin the enforcement of state or federal laws on constitutional grounds. Provision for three-judge courts has been retained, however, in reapportionment cases and where otherwise specifically required by an act of Congress, notably in voting-rights cases.

certiorari federal question issues in convictions in the state and federal systems and in all postconviction proceedings in those systems in which a conviction or a sentence is called into question."[11] Petitions for certiorari to the Supreme Court would be allowed when the national court of criminal appeals decided a case on the merits or when one or more of its members dissented from that court's denial of certiorari. The proposal could in theory eliminate a large percentage of the Supreme Court's cases, for the Court's applications caseload is today predominately a criminal one, and a substantial fraction of cases decided on the merits are also criminal.[12] But the effect of the Haynsworth solution in practice would depend on the new court's certiorari practices, on the degree of unanimity among the members of the court, and, most important, on the congruence between the new court and the Supreme Court on the questions of law raised by criminal defendants—all imponderables.

A particularly serious objection to the proposal is the fact that so many statutes carry both civil and criminal penalties for their violation. Which court would have the final say on questions of interpretation of such statutes? If it was the Supreme Court, then much of the workload-alleviating effect of the proposed new court might prove illusory.

3. *The Kurland Proposal.* □□ Another radical jurisdictional proposal is Professor Kurland's suggestion that the Supreme Court be limited to constitutional cases.[13] Approximately 66 percent of the cases on the Court's docket in the 1973 term raised constitutional issues.[14] Hence, limiting the Supreme Court to constitutional cases would have reduced by approximately 1,820 the number of

---

11. Clement F. Haynsworth, Jr., A New Court to Improve the Administration of Justice, 59 A.B.A.J. 841, 842 (1973).
12. See tables 3.2 and 4.10 *supra.*
13. Philip B. Kurland, Jurisdiction of the United States Supreme Court: Time for a Change? 59 Cornell L. Rev. 616, 628 (1974).
14. See table 3.11 *supra.*

cases filed in the 1973 term. Using the methods of calculating the time devoted to screening that underlie table 4.1,
we calculate that the elimination of these cases would have
saved the Court between 3.4 and 5.4 hours a week during
the 1973 term. Some of this time saving might have proved
illusory, however, since the Kurland proposal would give
litigants an even greater incentive than at present[15] to
characterize issues as constitutional in order to invoke the
Court's jurisdiction.

The greatest impact of Kurland's proposal would be on
the cases decided with full opinion: 54.7 percent of such
cases in the 1973 term involved constitutional issues.[16]
Some of these cases, to be sure, also involved nonconstitutional issues that the Court may have been anxious to
review. And some of what are now nonconstitutional cases
might reappear as constitutional cases if the Court's jurisdiction were limited to constitutional cases. Still, there
seems little doubt that the proposal would rid the Court of
a large number of time-consuming cases and also enable it
to review a larger number of constitutional cases than at
present. Thus the Kurland proposal would probably be a
more effective remedy for an excessive caseload than any
of the other proposals that are on the table. It also raises a
number of problems; for example, a new court would have
to be created to resolve definitively questions of federal
statutory law, for these would no longer be within the
Supreme Court's jurisdiction. The most difficult questions
raised by the proposal lie in the realm of the intangible.
Does the Court's responsibility to decide technical lawyers'
questions arising under various federal statutes, as well as
emotionally charged and politically resonant constitutional
questions, serve to discipline the Court's constitutional
adjudication—to make it more lawyer-like? If so, is this a
good thing? Conversely, does the Court's predominant
emphasis on constitutional adjudication affect, perhaps for

15. See p. 49 *supra.*
16. See table 4.9 *supra.*

the worse, the way in which it decides technical issues of
federal law—does it perhaps approach them in a political or
statesmanlike posture more suitable to constitutional
adjudication than to the resolution of technical lawyers'
questions? We are not sure that these questions are suscep-
tible of objective answers. That they must be answered to
evaluate the Kurland proposal is accordingly a serious draw-
back of that proposal. But for those—if only for those—
who believe that the Court's workload has reached crisis
proportions, the Kurland proposal deserves careful consideration.

4. *The Hufstedler Proposal.* □□ The American Bar
Association's Special Committee on Coordination of
Judicial Improvements has made a complex proposal (the
"Hufstedler proposal"), the consequences of which are
difficult to predict. The proposal is as follows:

> The key features of the proposed national court of appeals
> are these: (1) Congress creates a national court of appeals, (2)
> the judges of which are selected from active United States
> Circuit judges with not less than a specified number of years
> service, (3) it grants power to the Supreme Court, by Supreme
> Court rules, to confer jurisdiction on the new court, (4) within
> boundaries set by Congress, (5) to hear and to decide classes of
> litigation, or individual cases referred to it by the Supreme
> Court, and to recommend to the Supreme Court hearing or
> denial of hearings in such cases, (6) subject to the continuing
> power of the Supreme Court to accept or to reject any case for
> hearing, and further subject to the requirement, (7) that no
> decision of the national court shall become final until the lapse
> of a specified period of time after the records, decisions and
> recommendations of the national court have been received by
> the Supreme Court, and the Court has not taken active action
> thereon, (8) Congress creates new circuit judgeships to replace
> the circuit judges who will be assigned to the national court.[17]

This proposal would not reduce substantially the
Supreme Court's burden of initial review. Its potential lies,
rather, in enabling the Court to delegate decision on the
merits in certain categories of case to the national court of

---

17. Report of the ABA Special Committee on Coordination of Judicial
Improvements 3 (mimeograph, 1974).

appeals. In recent testimony before the Hruska commission, Judge Hufstedler suggested the following specific jurisdictional changes in implementation of the proposal: Congress would empower the Supreme Court to transfer to the national court of appeals (1) all tax cases, (2) all patent cases, (3) all petitions to review decisions of state courts of last resort in criminal cases, (4) petitions to review decisions of cases to which certain administrative agencies are parties (NLRB, SEC, FCC, FPC, ICC, and FAA), (5) nonconstitutional federal question conflicts between federal courts of appeals, and (6) categories specifically designated by Congress.[18]

The Hufstedler proposal would have a net effect on screening roughly similar to that of Kurland's constitutional court proposal. While Kurland's plan would eliminate roughly one-third of the new cases filed, the Hufstedler proposal would eliminate between 35 and 44 percent.[19] But the Hufstedler proposal—which in this respect is very different from Kurland's—provides only for "initial decision" by the new court. Supreme Court review of those decisions would remain possible. The total impact on the Court's workload would be uncertain.

5. *The Proposal of the Commission on Revision of the Federal Court Appellate System ("Hruska Commission").* □□ The proposals discussed thus far encountered considerable opposition. Apart from those critics who denied the existence of a workload problem, much of the opposition can be summarized in terms of the apprehension of many lawyers that they would lose access to the "one" Supreme

---

18. Statement of Shirley Hufstedler, Circuit Judge, United States Court of Appeals for the Ninth Circuit, to the Hruska Commission, Apr. 1, 1974, in Hearings Before the U.S. Commission on Revision of the Federal Court Appellate System, Second Phase, vol. 1, at 9 (preliminary print).

19. These figures are based on data for the 1972 and 1973 terms in table 3.11 for Kurland's proposal and in tables 3.3, 3.8, and 4.12 for Hufstedler's. The major "savings" under the latter proposal would result from the elimination of state criminal cases, for which reliable data are available; and a meaningful estimate can be made for the aggregate savings in the remaining areas of proposed jurisdictional change. The important points are the approximate magnitude and rough equality of the savings that might be effected by the two plans.

Court. There was even doubt expressed about the constitutionality of creating a "second" supreme court.[20] The proposal of the Hruska commission attempts to avoid these problems by proposing a national court of appeals that would decide *individual* cases referred to it by the Supreme Court rather than classes of cases (as envisaged by the Hufstedler proposal). The apparent origin of the Hruska commission proposal is an article by former Solicitor General Griswold,[21] although others, in particular Professor Black,[22] had suggested similar solutions. The recommendations of the Hruska commission have since been embodied in two Senate bills.[23]

S. 3423 proposes a national court of appeals composed of a chief judge and six associate judges. It would be located in Washington, D.C., though it might also "sit at such times and places within the United States as the court may designate." Cases would be heard en banc with five judges constituting a quorum.

Both the Hruska commission and S. 2762 provided for appointment of the judges by the president in accordance with the ordinary constitutional procedures. S. 3423 attempts to resolve the political problems inherent in giving a single president the opportunity to appoint the entire membership of so important a tribunal by substituting for presidential appointment in "one sitting" a three-stage appointment process.[24] At the establishment of the court

---

20. See Charles L. Black, Jr., The National Court of Appeals: An Unwise Proposal, 83 Yale L.J. 883, 885 (1974).

21. See Erwin N. Griswold, The Supreme Court's Case Load: Civil Rights and Other Problems, 1973 U. Ill. L.F. 615, and his Rationing Justice—The Supreme Court's Caseload and What the Court Does Not Do, 60 Cornell L. Rev. 335 (1975).

22. See Black, *supra* note 20, at 898.

23. S. 2762, 94th Cong., 1st Sess. (1975), was the original bill. An identical bill was introduced in the House by Representative Wiggins. H.R. 11218, 94th Cong., 1st Sess. (1975). Since its introduction, S. 2762 has been revised. The new bill carries the number S. 3423 and is printed in 122 Cong. Rec., at S6985 (daily ed. May 12, 1976). All of our references are to S. 3423 unless otherwise indicated.

24. See remarks of Senator Hruska, 122 Cong. Rec., at S6987 (daily ed. May 12, 1976).

the then-president would appoint two judges; another two would be appointed exactly four years later; and after another four-year period the last three judges would be chosen. In the meantime, the full complement of seven judges would be reached by taking, in the first stage, the five most senior circuit judges willing to serve who were not yet eligible for retirement and would not become eligible during the first four-year period, and, in the second stage, the three most senior circuit judges who were qualified according to the foregoing criteria.

This means that it would take eight years for the court to achieve a regular membership, and if we understand the scheme correctly it also means that during the eight-year period the court would see 15 new faces, barring additional turnover due to death, resignation, and other unforeseen termination: 7 new faces in the first stage, 5 new faces in the second stage (2 regular appointments plus the 3 then most senior circuit judges), and 3 new faces in the third stage (3 regular appointments). And by the end of eight years, some of the original regular appointees would no doubt have left the court for reasons of age, ill health, etc. This instability of judicial tenure seems a recipe for legal uncertainty, which by the analysis in chapter 3 could be expected to generate additional litigation that might ultimately increase the Supreme Court's caseload.

As originally conceived by the Hruska commission, the national court of appeals was to have two different jurisdictions: a "reference" jurisdiction and a "transfer" jurisdiction. The transfer jurisdiction was to consist of cases transferred to the new court by the courts of appeals, the Court of Claims, and the Court of Customs and Patent Appeals. Opposition to this feature was so strong[25] that it was dropped from S. 3423.

The reference jurisdiction would consist of cases referred to the new court by the Supreme Court after that Court had (1) denied certiorari or (2) decided to refer the

---

25. See *id.* at S6986.

case instead of noting probable jurisdiction of an appeal. The Supreme Court could, and in cases subject to review by appeal "shall," direct the national court of appeals to decide any case so referred. As summarized by the Hruska commission the referral jurisdiction would work as follows:

Petitions for Certiorari. The Supreme Court could decide:

(1) to retain the case and render a decision on the merits:
(2) to deny certiorari without more, thus terminating the litigation;
(3) to deny certiorari and refer the case to the National Court of Appeals for that court to decide on the merits;
(4) to deny certiorari and refer the case to the National Court, giving that court discretion either to decide the case on the merits, or to deny review and thus terminate the litigation.[26]

Appeals. The Supreme Court could decide:

(1) to retain the case and render a decision on the merits; or
(2) to refer the case to the National Court for decision on the merits.[27]

Neither S. 3423 nor the Hruska commission purports to prescribe the procedures of the Supreme Court except that the commission stated its premise "that the rules for the grant or denial of certiorari would remain as they are."[28] Thus, it would presumably take six votes (the number now required for denying certiorari) to refer a case.

The first thing to be noted concerning the reference jurisdiction is that it would not reduce the screening burden on the Supreme Court. On the contrary, it might well increase it. At present the Court has only to decide whether to take a case or not. The additional options created by the reference jurisdiction would require additional and difficult evaluations where the decision is now to deny. Is the case sufficiently meritorious to be referred?

---

26. Commission on Revision of the Federal Court Appellate System, Structure and Internal Procedures: Recommendations for Change 32-33 (Washington, D.C., June 1975) [hereinafter cited as Hruska commission].
27. *Id.* at 33.
28. *Id.*

Should it be referred with directions to be decided on the merits? How will the national court resolve the substantive issues? A Supreme Court Justice might have to ask himself how referral would affect his own views concerning the merits. For instance, a Justice might regularly vote to deny certiorari in a class of cases because he believed the majority would not resolve the issue in a satisfactory manner. For him a "rational" reference decision might require a prediction of the likely outcome in the national court and of the attitude the Supreme Court would take subsequent to a decision by the national court. The screening function would thus assume greater importance, which would make it more difficult to discharge and therefore more time consuming.

S. 3423 and the commission apparently assume that the present unsatisfactory state of affairs concerning appeals (in the technical sense) will continue. The commission was worried—rightly so, in our opinion—by the extremely tenuous precedential value attaching to summary dispositions.[29] Although the commission did not discuss its recommended solution in any detail, the bill, which would give the Supreme Court the opportunity to refer ("may refer") an appeal to the new court "in lieu of noting probable jurisdiction," would apparently offer the Supreme Court three choices: (1) to dispose of an appeal summarily; (2) to note probable jurisdiction; (3) to refer the appeal to the national court with directions to decide. In the 1974 term, 255 appeals were filed with the Supreme Court, and during the same term the Court disposed of only 53 appeals after oral argument.[30] If the Supreme Court were to refer to the national court a substantial portion of those appeals that it now decides in a plenary way, plus a signifi-

---

29. *Id.* at 6.

30. Information supplied by Office of the Clerk, United States Supreme Court. The enactment of Pub. L. No. 94-381 (see note 10 *supra*) as this monograph goes to press alters somewhat the context of our analysis, but only in such a way as to weaken one of the arguments for the creation of a new national court by reducing the Supreme Court's formally obligatory jurisdiction.

cant number of the appeals now disposed of summarily (so as to remedy the deficiencies of the present system), the national court would immediately find its own docket crowded with appeals. There would be little room left for certiorari cases (assuming the new court could not be expected to decide more than roughly 120 cases a year). If this development did *not* occur, the new state of affairs would hardly be an improvement; summary dispositions would continue to have their uncertain value—unless Congress did away with all or most appeals. And if Congress did drastically restrict appeals, a major argument in favor of the new court would be removed.

Under S. 3423 "any case in the National Court of Appeals may be reviewed by the Supreme Court by writ of certiorari granted upon the petition of any party to any such case before or after rendition of judgment or decree." There is no way of predicting in what percentage of the national court's decisions a petition for certiorari would be filed with the Supreme Court and how often the Supreme Court would grant certiorari. However, in view of the high initial turnover on the new court and the consequent difficulty of developing stable working relations with the Supreme Court, it seems unlikely that the bill would achieve, at least for 10-12 years, the goal of its sponsors "to increase the capacity of the Federal Judicial system for definitive adjudication of issues of national law."[31]

There is reason to believe that even after completion of stage three the Supreme Court might be forced to review numerous decisions by the new court. Judge Friendly has stressed the problem of conscience a Justice of the Supreme Court would be faced with:

> When he is confronted with a decision of the National Court which he tentatively thinks to be wrong, refusal to exercise his powers would mean that he was allowing bad law to be made on a nationwide basis and with no possibility of subsequent disagreement. . . . Beyond this, I predict that as a practical mat-

---

31. 122 Cong. Rec., at S6986 (daily ed. May 12, 1976) (remarks of Senator Hruska).

ter, the Justices will simply not refrain from reviewing decisions, especially divided decisions, of the National Court on any
issue of real importance even though they were willing to let
the National Court have a first crack at them.[32]

Moreover, apart from the particularly acute problems of
the new court in its formative period, the court would
never add any substantial certainty to the law because even
denials of certiorari by the Supreme Court in the second
round would leave the Damocles sword of a future change
of mind by the Supreme Court hanging over the new court.
In these circumstances we find it difficult to believe that
the national court would substantially relieve the Court's
merits docket. Given that the new court would *add* to the
screening task, the proposal seems dubious in the extreme.

B.   Some Alternative Approaches

1. Screening. □□ We estimate that roughly one working day per week is devoted by each Justice to screening
the applications for review, which now average about 4,000
a year. None of the proposals that have received substantial
public attention—none of the proposals, that is, discussed in
the previous part of this chapter—seems effectively designed
to lighten this burden materially. Perhaps so long as the
screening function remains a part of the Court's responsibilities one cannot expect a substantial reduction in the
one-day-a-week figure—it may be the irreducible minimum
given the volume of the nation's federal legal business.
Moreover, since screening occupies by our estimate only
about 20 percent of the Justices' time, even substantial
reductions in the amount of time devoted to screening
would not produce dramatic reductions in the total workload of the Court. For example, a 20 percent reduction in
the amount of time that the Justices devote to screening
would produce an overall time saving of only 4 percent.

Law clerk time is another matter. Substantial savings in

---

32. Letter from Henry J. Friendly to A. Leo Levin, Apr. 22, 1975, in
Hearings, *supra* note 18, vol. 2, at 1313.

the clerk time devoted to the screening function could be obtained by extending the "pool" system described in the last chapter. Five Justices now participate in the pool, and with 3 law clerks assigned to each Justice, the pool makes available 15 clerks for the roughly 4,000 cases now filed each year—which amounts to some 270 petitions per clerk instead of the 1,330 that each would have if 3 clerks performed the prescreening function for each Justice individually. Since a majority of the Justices will hire the fourth clerk authorized for the 1976 term, there will be a further substantial decrease in clerk time spent on screening except for those Justices who do not participate in the pool and/or will not avail themselves of a fourth clerk. While these arrangements do not, of course, affect the screening time of the small minority of Justices who do most of the screening themselves, these Justices now have a considerable amount of clerk time available for other forms of assistance precisely because they do the screening themselves.

The long and short of these calculations is that the source of the workload problem is *not* screening. And if 20 percent of Justice time spent on screening is deemed excessive, alternatives other than relieving the Supreme Court as a whole of some of its caseload are available. One doubtless unpalatable possibility would be to charge much higher filing fees in nonindigent cases. Another, suggested by Kurland (who was repeating an idea put forward in 1927 by Frankfurter and Landis), is to divide the screening function equally among the nine Justices.[33] Vesting that much authority in a single Justice is too radical a proposal for many to accept, but what we find less understandable is why the notion of *panels* is also rejected out of hand.[34]

Panels of three judges each have long been used by the German Constitutional Court, apparently successfully. That court is divided into two "Senates" (each with jurisdiction over different areas of constitutional law). The caseload of

---

33. Kurland, *supra* note 13, at 630.
34. See, *e.g.,* Paul A. Freund, A National Court of Appeals, 25 Hastings L.J. 1301, 1305 (1974).

the entire court averages roughly 1,750 cases a year[35] (a figure which, incidentally, has remained quite stable for many years). Given that the West German population is roughly one-third of the United States' and that the German court is restricted to constitutional cases, 1,750 is a large number of cases.

Most of these cases—96 percent—come to the court in the form of so-called constitutional complaints, a form of action that is free of court cost and does not require counsel (34 percent of complainants to the First Senate were unrepresented in 1967).[36] The constitutional complaint is the functional equivalent of our petition for certiorari, but it is subject to a different screening procedure. After a complaint has been lodged with the court it is sent to the Senate that has jurisdiction. There it is first screened by a panel of three judges who can unanimously reject the complaint.[37] But if one judge votes to accept, the complaint then goes to the full Senate. Rejected complaints need not be accompanied by any written justification although more than half of the complaints rejected by the panels of the Second Senate in 1971 were accompanied by short opinions.[38] From 1956 through 1971 only 3.8 percent of the complaints survived the panel screening (a figure roughly equal to the grant rate for indigent petitions in the Supreme Court).[39]

The German panel procedure is not without its difficulties. The most serious is that assignments of judges to the three panels are neither temporary nor random. In the past this has led to panel "practices" not always in accord with the views of a Senate majority. The rules of the court now provide that the composition of the panels shall not

---

35. Donald P. Kommers, Judicial Politics in West Germany 163-67, tables 8 & 9.

36. *Id.* at 168.

37. Gesetz über das Bundesverfassungsgericht sec. 93a, revised text of Feb. 3, 1971, [1971] BGBl. I 105.

38. Kommers, *supra* note 35, at 169.

39. See note 1, chapter 4, *supra.*

remain unchanged for more than three years.[40] The second difficulty has to do with the German system of reporting decisions, which is not complete. Unless published by the complainant or his attorney, rejections often remain unknown to the general public and the bar. Occasionally, the judges themselves are not too well informed about the decision practice of other panels, and this creates a danger that conflicts among panels will remain unnoticed.

If the Supreme Court were to screen by means of panels (each of, say, three Justices), one would assume that American notions of fairness would dictate complete randomization and panel rotation on a case-by-case basis. This might still lead to denials where now there are grants. But since a single Justice could bring a case to the entire Court, few such instances would occur. At worst a panel would sometimes be able to prevent the Court from deciding a particular case. But an important issue would, of course, recur in other cases.

According to Justice Brennan, at present roughly one-fourth of all applications for review are put on the Court's "discuss list" by one or more Justices.[41] If one assumes that under a panel system 20 percent of all cases would be placed on the list and further that each of the Justices would already be familiar (as a panelist) with roughly one-third of those cases, the panel system would have the effect of cutting a Justice's screening task roughly in half, producing a saving of approximately one-half working day a week. That there would be substantially more "errors" under such procedure is not intuitively plausible.

This alternative is, of course, radical in the sense that only three votes would be needed where it now takes six to turn down a petition. In order to accommodate the rare major issue that is not easily duplicated, or where there is a potential interest in immediate resolution among Justices

---

40. Geschäftsordnung des Bundesverfassungsgerichts sec. 38.
41. William J. Brennan, Jr., The National Court of Appeals: Another Dissent, 40 U. Chi. L. Rev. 473, 480 (1973).

not on the panel to which the case has been assigned, the procedure could be modified to allow any Justice to join any of the panels if he so desired. We do not assume, however, that there would be a great need for such a safety valve. We believe that panels, under guidelines issued by the Court, could be trusted to make their decisions not with an eye to their personal predilections but fairly and in terms of the worthiness of a case for Supreme Court review (which would include predictions about views of the other Justices); for the Justices comprise a small group and have a strong incentive to behave cooperatively with one another.

But, in summary, we repeat that we do not believe that the Court's workload problem centers on screening. We offer the foregoing alternative only to broaden the discussion and to stimulate the imaginations of those students of the workload problem who take a graver view of the burdens of the screening function than do we.

2. Dispositions on the Merits. □□ The Hruska commission and other proponents of radical change in the Supreme Court's structure or jurisdiction assume that at present too few important cases are being resolved authoritatively for the nation as a whole. They ascribe this to caseload pressures, but their assumption can be evaluated independently of assigning a cause to it. It is extremely difficult to determine the desirable number of national decisions. As our previous discussion of conflicts among circuits showed, the number of serious conflicts among circuits that remain unresolved in the short run is apparently no more than 25-45 a year. If one takes the position that some, perhaps most, of these conflicts may actually be desirable from the vantage point of circuit "federalism" (the gathering of experience with various interpretations of federal law),[42] the problem may not seem urgent. According to the surveys conducted by the Hruska commission

---

42. See pp. 86-87 *supra*.

itself, among the "consumers" of national law only the patent bar is distinctly unhappy about the present state of affairs; and, as Judge Friendly has suggested, differing opinions about patentability "will no more be ended by occasional references of patent cases to the National Court"[43] than they have been by the Supreme Court itself.

The answer to the patent problem probably lies in a patent court rather than in more decisions by another court of "generalists"; and in our opinion the same is true of tax conflicts. During the 1971-1973 terms an average of 85 tax cases a year were filed with the Supreme Court, and of these the Court decided half a dozen or so a year with full opinion.[44] The argument for a court of tax appeals rests on grounds independent of the Supreme Court's capacity to resolve tax issues: it makes as much or more sense in terms of alleviating the burdens on the circuit courts and generally doing away with incongruities in our system of tax litigation.[45] We do not believe that the establishment of a court of tax appeals would deprive the Supreme Court of exposure to matters it should know about in order to discharge its other responsibilities or that a specialized court would be jurisprudentially less capable of dealing with these matters than a court of general jurisdiction. It should be made clear, however, that on the basis of our data we cannot conclude that a patent court or a court of tax appeals would significantly affect either the Supreme Court's screening docket or its merits docket.

Putting patent and tax cases to one side, and assuming, if only for the sake of argument, that the Supreme Court today is resolving too few conflicts, the solution may not lie in an additional court but in greater selectivity on the part of the Supreme Court with regard to cases *not* involving conflicts. Is Supreme Court intervention in newly emerging areas of legal controversy warranted in the

---

43. Testimony in Hearings, *supra* note 18, vol. 2, at 1315.
44. See tables 3.2 & 4.11 *supra.*
45. See H. Todd Miller, Comment: A Court of Tax Appeals Revisited, 85 Yale L.J. 228 (1975).

absence of a conflict among lower courts? Is it not prima facie premature to resolve definitively a controversy that has not yet been litigated enough times to generate a split among the circuits or the state supreme courts? Why, in short, should not conflict cases comprise the major component of the Court's merits docket? The fact that according to our data a conflict is not even alleged in two-thirds of the applications for review on the appellate docket[46] suggests that the Court could reduce the number of cases it accepts for review without impairing its effective functioning as the head of the federal judicial system. Thus, even if one accepted Mr. Justice White's suggestion that a merits docket of 100 cases is all the Court is competent to handle,[47] the Court would still have adequate capacity to decide all cases in which the public interest requires *immediate* resolution rather than permits a longer "experience gathering" period in the lower courts.

There are other ways in which the Court's workload could be reduced without substantial cost. It could employ panels for hearing cases on the merits (rather than merely in the screening process as discussed earlier). The German two-Senates model has worked smoothly, by and large, and while the division of labor between the Senates is based on jurisdictional allocations not easily transferable to the United States,[48] a panel system based on somewhat different jurisdictional divisions is conceivable for our Supreme Court. Our data would make it possible to estimate the panel caseloads resulting from whatever jurisdictional differentiation was adopted. We shall not pursue this alternative because we believe that the opposition to it is probably insurmountable, even though many of the arguments advanced against panels (for instance, the potential for conflict among them) are unpersuasive.[49]

---

46. See table 4.12 *supra.*
47. See Hruska commission, *supra* note 26, at 34.
48. See Kommers, *supra* note 35, at 102.
49. The German experience suggests that conflicts have been infrequent. And mechanisms for en banc adjudication make it possible to control the

Perhaps a more realistic solution would be to limit decision by panel to those cases on the "discuss list" that the Court determines, as a matter of first impression, to be noncontroversial.[50] At present roughly 25 percent of all decisions with full opinion are unanimous.[51] If, let us say, only five Justices were assigned to hear cases, in which a preliminary review indicated unanimity, the average number of mertis cases that each Justice considered would be reduced by approximately 11 percent (*i.e.,* 4/9 x .25). This is a significant reduction, albeit mainly in the decision of the easier cases on the merits docket; but it does imply a somewhat more elaborate and therefore time-consuming screening process.

An alternative to panels for dealing with noncontroversial cases is shorter opinions or a more frequent use of per curiams. The average length of majority opinions doubled between 1969 and 1974,[52] yet there is no indication that the difficulty of the average case increased in that interval. In cases where the Court is unanimous, relatively short per curiams should be the rule. Furthermore, as regular observers of the Court, we cannot share the implicit view of the Justices that the average dissenting opinion calls for a 2,000 word essay.[53] No doubt much of the writing burden actually rests on the law clerks, but we know from our own experience in reviewing student work how time consuming the reviewing task is if conscientiously performed.

There are other steps the Court could take in dealing with the merits docket. At present approximately 180 hours a term, or roughly 4.5 hours a week (assuming a

---

problem effectively, as is done in the federal courts of appeals, where decision by panel is, of course, the norm.

50. Cf. Nathan Lewin, Helping the Court with Its Work, New Republic, Mar. 3, 1973, at 15, 19.

51. This estimate is based on figures appearing in the annual Supreme Court surveys of the *Harvard Law Review* (November issue).

52. See table 4.7 *supra.*

53. See *id.*

40-week term), are spent in oral argument.[54] Given the low average quality of oral argument in the Supreme Court, it seems possible that there are a good number of cases that could be just as well decided on the briefs.[55] In Germany oral argument is the rare exception even in cases decided with full opinion. While this is not an ideal state of affairs either, we are unable to perceive a difference in the quality of opinions that can be attributed to the lack of oral argument in the German court. Neither extreme—no oral argument or oral argument in every case—is clearly more meritorious than the other. The federal courts of appeals no longer hear oral argument in every case. The Supreme Court could learn from them.

The most effective method of reducing the number of cases filed with the Court that is wholly within the Court's power to effectuate would be the formulation and publication of detailed guidelines regarding the criteria for granting the denying review. There are no criteria at present, other than the fatuous generalities recited in the Court's rules[56] and opinions.[57] The Court should indicate clearly the classes of cases in which the likelihood of a grant of review is so slight as to make the preparation and filing of a petition for certiorari a waste of the litigant's time and money. Simply publishing the percentage of cases in which review is granted within various subject-matter areas would be a useful first step.

This suggests a larger point: the passivity of the present Supreme Court with respect to the formulation of solutions to the alleged workload problem. In light of the grave doubts about the wisdom or practicality of the Hruska commission proposal, the burden is now upon the Court itself to propose a solution, if indeed a majority of the

---

54. See table 4.4 *supra*.
55. See Lewin, *supra* note 50, at 19.
56. U.S. Sup. Ct. R. 19.
57. See, *e.g.,* Cort v. Ash, 422 U.S. 66, 74 (1975); Blue Chip Stamps v. Manor Drug Stores, 421 U.S. 723, 727 (1975); United Housing Foundation Inc. v. Foreman, 421 U.S. 837, 847 (1975).

Justices believe that the problem has reached serious proportions. In a manner very different from the role played
by the Taft Court in the formulation and enactment of the
Judges' Bill (the Judiciary Act of 1925),[58] the present
Supreme Court has failed to produce any proposals of its
own. Perhaps its first order of business should be to consti-
tute a study group from among its own members, or to
assemble as a committee of the whole, for the purpose of
devising solutions supported by a consensus of its members.
We believe that, to a larger extent than realized so far, the
business of the Supreme Court is also the Supreme Court's
business.

C.   Conclusion

On the basis of the statistical analysis in previous chapters, we are not persuaded that the Supreme Court's workload has reached the point at which radical changes in the
Court's jurisdiction or in the structure of federal appellate
review should be contemplated—especially since far more
modest reforms, many desirable in their own right regardless of workload pressures, have yet to be implemented.
Cumulatively, these reforms could, if not solve the problem, at least postpone the moment when a permanent
solution must be found, to allow time for additional
study—which, judging by the quality of the proposals thus
far advanced, is desperately needed.

The modest reforms that we endorse include the aboli-
tion of the remaining obligatory jurisdiction of the
Supreme Court and of direct appeals to the Court from
federal district courts, the creation of supreme courts of
patent and tax appeals, greater pooling of law clerks for
screening applications for review, reduction in the number
of concurring and dissenting opinions, denial or curtailment
of oral argument in some cases, greater use of short per
curiam opinions to decide unanimous cases, and the

---

58. See pp. 19-20 *supra.*

promulgation of detailed guidelines regarding the criteria for the grant and denial of review. No doubt each of these proposals requires greater elaboration than we have attempted here. Our allegiance to them is therefore tentative rather than final. The important point is the desirability of shifting the focus of the policy debate from far-reaching proposals to more limited reforms that seem more appropriate to the nature of the problem as elucidated in this monograph.